Edda Armstrong

1984

The
Sweater Workshop

Jacqueline Fee

to

Elizabeth

"Things must be right in themselves, and good for use."
Eric Gill, English. 1882–1940

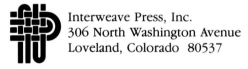

Interweave Press, Inc.
306 North Washington Avenue
Loveland, Colorado 80537

The excerpt from Knitting at the Top *by Barbara
Walker, is reprinted with the permission of Charles
Scribner's Sons. Copyright ©1972 Barbara G.
Walker.*

Photography © Joe A. Coca, 1983.

Library of Congress Catalog Number 83-080246
ISBN: 0-934026-12-2

ACKNOWLEDGEMENTS

First, I must express a very special thank you to my daughter, Nancy. Her love of early textiles and her pursuit of their reproduction filled our home with old looms and wheels, and our lives with weavers and spinners. This association with true creators made me want to hide my knitting. It became suddenly unsatisfying, and took on an air of inferiority; it seemed a copycat craft, akin to painting by numbers. The question began to nag, "Why don't knitters knit as spinners spin, as weavers weave, or, even, as quilters quilt, as potters pot, as sculptors sculpt, with a choice of materials and a few guidelines to follow?" The answer? There were precious few guidelines—no book of blank stitches. You now have it. The bare bones; skeletons of sweaters to knit of any yarn, and to embellish until your heart's content.

To another Nancy, Nancy Latady, thank you for being there and guiding me through my first wheel turnings; and, to my hand-spun yarn itself, for not conforming to the gauge of another.

Subsequently, to each talented member of our South Shore Spinner's Guild—collectively for energy and enthusiasm, individually for encouragement. And, most grateful thanks to one particular talent in that group, Patricia LaLiberte, for her very special kindness in rendering the charming stitch illustrations.

Thanks also to Connie Pearlstein, my Devil's Advocate on the West Coast, and to Anne Gould, Jeanne Haviland, Marlies Price, and Toni Trudell, her counterparts on the East, for reading, testing, and commenting.

To Miriam Chesley and Linda Lincoln—thank you for always listening.

And, to my students, from that first adventurous six—Debby Blanchard, Pat Curtin, Jean Dionne, Carolyn McKenna, Kathleen Ouellette, and Elizabeth Reardon—to all those who have followed, I am indebted to every one of you; you are all here in the pages of this book. You were its inspiration.

To Linda Ligon, my editor, for recognizing the need of rescuing knitting and knitters from a seeming fate.

And finally, to the rest of my family, to my husband Peter, for his thoughtfulness, help, and patient understanding; to my son John, who sent good thoughts from college in New York; and, even to dog, Gus, for waiting all those minutes.

Love, and thank you, all.

CONTENTS

INTRODUCTION
THE SWEATER SAMPLER

EQUIP YOURSELF

UNRAVEL YOUR THINKING

THE BASIC SWEATER

THE SWEATER VARIATIONS

INTRODUCTION

From yarn shop to supermarket, you, the knitter, are confronted with various species of patterns for sweaters: sweaters designed by others for you to work to their specifications, the trend of the knitting industry today. This book veers from the current trend. It is a retreat from dependence upon others, an alternative for you who wish to knit sweaters on your own. This retreat begins in the literal sense of the word. It means taking a giant step back to the first cast-on stitch and thoughtfully working step by step through construction possibilities. By so doing, you will become an independent, *thinking* knitter. Your reward will be perfect fitting, perfectly constructed seamless sweaters, knit of any yarn you choose.

The Sweater Workshop contains no specifics, a detail your sharp eye may have noticed. Yarns are not stipulated; the customary comparison chart is missing; needle sizes are not recommended; gauge is not prescribed; and there are no columns of sizes and numbers (some in parentheses).

The elimination of these restrictions allows you to design a sweater in an atmosphere of creativity, and with a spirit of adventure. The most enjoyable aspect of this release from rigid attention to printed instructions is the freedom to select the yarn of your choice. The energy conscious and the fashion conscious may select yarns for snug, warm shelters, or designer adaptations. The handspinner may create a spectacular original with those skeins of handspun that defy categorization; and, the weaver is, at last, granted the intelligence to knit a sweater that will be a smashing match for her handwoven skirt. Whether the yarn is handspun or millspun, cotton or wool, thick or thin, its selection is your prerogative.

To knit in this mode using any desired yarn, a gauge sample is a necessity. Though now you may regard this exercise as a dull chore, in the future, as you are accustomed to knitting on your own, it will become second nature and an exciting excuse for experimentation. In fact, and properly defined, a gauge sample is a sample piece of fabric, a preview of the delightful sweater to come.

"Gauge Page" replaces the usual number systems and provides you with an individual formula for each sweater. The arithmetic is simple and is based on your sample's stitches to the inch and your preferred sweater measurements. Each sweater deserves its own Gauge Page, and you may want to add more specific information, such as yarn type, date, recipient, pattern stitch and so forth. Kept in a notebook, with samples attached, these pages are a permanent record of projects undertaken, or to be undertaken; a memory book, if you will. If organized papers are not your cup of tea, and, if you write small, Gauge Page can be reduced to a hang tag, or further reduced to one number on file in your head.

The format of *The Sweater Workshop* is the result of years of practical application in classes and workshops attended by novice and veteran knitters of every age, race, color, creed, and sex. Its division into three segments, "The Sweater Sampler," "The Basic Sweater," and "Basic Sweater Variations," has naught to do with your ability and experience as a knitter, but to the success of your sweaters. Therefore, this book, as any book, starts on Page 1—for all. It is first a guide to lead you through the actual mechanics of the processes, and second, it is a manual to be used over and over as you vary its component parts. The directions do presuppose that you can knit and purl.

The Sweater Sampler most certainly fits the general definition of a sampler: a piece of ornamental needlework made as an exhibition of skill. Ornamental it is, not with bobbles and cables but with good, sound, tried and true construction techniques; the pick of the crop, especially selected for sweater knitting. It incorporates all the skills needed for any sweater you will ever want to design and knit. This unusual piece is a much loved accomplishment of knitters at all levels of ability. No one is excused from working it.

In essence, the sampler is a sweater worked from the bottom up and in the round, as is The Basic Sweater to follow. Thus, its correlation to that sweater is obvious. The sampler paces, in sequence, the options available to you for fit, styling, and originality. Instructions are given for the mechanics of each technique. More important than the mechanics, you will become aware of the peculiar characteristics of stitch combinations. This awareness comes from knitting one after the other, in the same piece of work, not in isolated squares unrelated to each other. A comparison can be made, and the best combination selected for use in a particular situation. The sampler is an original concept, its contents gathered and culled from a myriad of sources throughout many knitting years. Most are common knowledge techniques assembled with a sense of order and meaning; some are of my own invention, and some are borrowed with kind permission.

For the principles of The Basic Sweater I owe a debt of gratitude to Elizabeth Zimmerman and her nemesis, the purl stitch. Tucked in her book, *Knitting Without Tears,* is a raglan sweater of pure, logical construction—a masterpiece of fabrication. Worked to one's own gauge by percentages, the sweater develops proportionally to any size. With Elizabeth's very kind permission, the basic sweater presented here is an adaptation of hers. This version varies somewhat; most noticeably, the neckline has been lowered and shaped to a true crew neck. Those of you who have knit this sweater previously should work it again. Those of you who haven't, must. For this basic sweater is the proving ground, and its mastery will provide you with the framework for many a variation. A clear understanding of its construction and the concept of Gauge Page will stir your imagination for other sweater designs, and make it possible for you to knit them.

The Basic Sweater Variations developed as the result of Elizabeth's inspirational sweater. The motivation was compelling to knit another and another from its mold. Offered here, in this section, are directions for varying the neckline, and for varying the style from a pullover to a cardigan. Then, if in an appropriate pattern, either style may be worn inside out, a tribute to the sweater's pure and simple seamless construction.

In summary, *The Sweater Workshop* is a viewpoint. Its aim is to cause you to take an analytical look at sweater knitting with your yarn as the starting point. As you work through the progressive steps, my hope is that you will come to realize the satisfaction of knitting on your own. The purpose of this book is to hint at potentialities, to stimulate your ideas, and to foster a keen appreciation for the knitted fabric.

No effort has been made to present novelties. Rather, great care has been taken to present selections that you may interpret and develop. Through choice, you, the knitter, as any fine craftsman, may strive for originality, quality, and perfection. Your gain will be a true sense of achievement.

Think knitting,
J.M.F.

cast-off in ribbing

lacing round

plain hem

Swiss darning

two-color knitting

decreases

raised stripe

purl stripe

knitted cord

knit stripe

sweatshirt pocket

increases

stripe in ribbing

knitted belt

K2, P2 ribbing

twisted rib

K1, P1 ribbing

stockinette stitch

garter stitch

The sweater sampler—front view.

THE SWEATER SAMPLER

The sampler is your opportunity to experience the whys, the wheres, and the whens of knitting a sweater. As you work from stitch to stitch exploring the more obvious how-to's, this underlying focus becomes apparent; reason emerges as the key to a perfectly constructed sweater. Combine this perspective with your own wits, wisdom, and natural flair, and you have the makings of many a variation. And varied they will be, for timidity and hesitation will be gone. Proudly, and without a second thought, you'll be adding a pocket here, a bit of lace there. This new "nothing-to-it" attitude will spark your enthusiasm for knitting.

To stir your imagination even more, why not make a fresh new start? Before getting underway with the sampler, organize a knitting niche. Search the house. Poke through the many bags and baskets. Gather all your knitting gear together: the yarns, the needles, and the books. (With luck, you may find the sampler makings, or enough yarn for a sweater or two.) Then, confiscate a chest of drawers, a wicker hamper, or a trunk—think big. Station this windfall beside your favorite chair, and add a good light. Your space is defined; settle in with contentment. Oh, just one last thing before you sit down—you'll need some paper and a pencil. Not only for your hen-scratchings, but primarily for a list—a list of who wants what sweater, of what yarn, with what pocket where. Your hands will never be idle again.

Now, for the sampler you will need:

Yarn. Use a *light color* 4-ply knitting worsted weight yarn, the common ordinary garden variety. Dark shades obscure technique; a blessing sometimes, but not advantageous in the sampler. One 4 ounce skein is ample, or, as so many have shrunk to 3½, that amount will just do it. Ply is more important than price, so whether it is 100% virgin orlon, or 100% virgin wool, be sure the four strands are twisted together tightly, else you will spend too much time dealing with split stitches. You will also need about an ounce of yarn in a contrasting color; those new-found scraps are fine as long as they are approximately the diameter of the base yarn.

Needles. The sampler is worked on a 16″ circular needle; metal, if you can possibly find one, in size #6, or #7, or #8—whichever is most comfortable for you with your yarn. Find a set of double-pointed needles in about the same size, one fine double-pointed needle, two stray buttons, the few items listed in Miscellany*, and that's it. You're ready to start.

Format. The directions for the sampler are specifically written for right-hand knitters. You left-hand knitters have your own wonderful ways of working the yarn and the needles, and should have no problem translating the yarn positions from right to left. If a specific right-hand technique is impracticable, such as cast-on, substitute your own best left-hand method.

The sampler is worked basically in the round. However, directions for flat knitting are also included, where applicable, for the day you knit a cardigan, or start the neck shaping in a pullover—a move that requires back and forth knitting from that moment on. In the few instances where both round and flat directions are given, keep an eagle eye out for, and on, the ROUND—that is the method to follow in the sampler.

Carefully read through the comment and the ROUND method for each technique before following the actual instructions that will take you through the sampler. In no time at all, you will have completed your sampler and assembled the skills for many a sweater on your own.

Good luck and enjoy! Hold it high when you're through for all to admire—and tell anyone who will listen what it all means. Then tuck it beside you for reference, or better still, hide it. Embroidery samplers seem to endure a haughty fate, lovingly framed and carefully hung, but this one has a tendency to walk by you on a leg, to hang by the chimney (with care), or to prance about as a puppet with eyes above its afterthought mouth. On great insistence, it may lead to a mate for sleeves, or with the addition of feet, the fanciest pair of stockings in town. And, who knows, it might even wind up warming a cold fish. But, after all, isn't turn about fair play? If it weren't for fish, would the sweater exist? What will ''they'' think in 200 years—a windsock, an urn cozy, a . . .?

*Miscellany, p. 67.

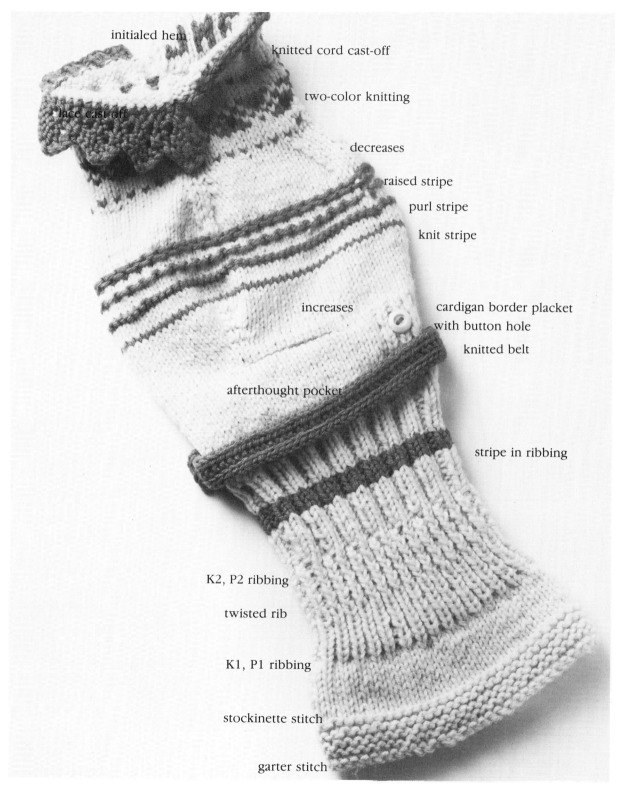

initialed hem

knitted cord cast-off

two-color knitting

lace cast-off

decreases

raised stripe

purl stripe

knit stripe

increases

cardigan border placket
with button hole

knitted belt

afterthought pocket

stripe in ribbing

K2, P2 ribbing

twisted rib

K1, P1 ribbing

stockinette stitch

garter stitch

The sweater sampler—back view.

The Cable Cast-on

The cable cast-on, as its name implies, resembles a smooth cable or rope of yarn, and significant to an inside-out sweater, it is reversible. More important, it is strong and elastic. In a sweater constructed from the bottom up, the cast-on automatically becomes the base of the body and sleeve ribbing. As part of the ribbing, this row, or round, must have give. Otherwise, the elasticity of the ribbing will be restricted, the edge will wear from stress and strain, and the whole sweater will feel uncomfortable.

The cable cast-on guarantees the correct tension; the spacing of the stitches forces looseness.

METHOD:

1st Stitch—Make a slip knot leaving a good 6″ tail of yarn. Insert one end of the 16″ circular needle through the loop of the slip knot, and adjust the loop to fit the needle by pulling down on the ends of the yarn. This first stitch is on the left needle. The slip knot gives easily to insert the right needle.

2nd Stitch—Insert the right needle into the slip knot stitch as if to knit.
• Take the yarn around the right needle as if to knit.
• Pull the loop through, but do not drop the slip knot stitch off the left needle.
• Insert the left needle straight down into the center of the loop.

This straight down move may be a change if you have previously used the knitting-on method and inserted the left needle from under the loop, thus twisting the stitch before putting it on the left needle. That move tightened the stitch to avoid a row of holes. For the cable cast-on, the stitch must not be twisted. To repeat, insert the left needle straight down into the center of the loop.

• Pull *gently* on the yarn as you transfer the loop to the left needle.
Do not let the second stitch snuggle up to the slip knot stitch—keep good distance between them.

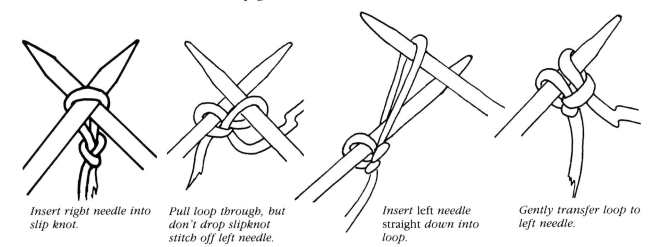

Insert right needle into slip knot.

Pull loop through, but don't drop slipknot stitch off left needle.

Insert left *needle* straight *down into loop.*

Gently transfer loop to left needle.

3rd Stitch—Insert the right needle *between* the first and second stitches. Yes, right smack out *between* the two.
• Take the yarn around as if to knit.
• Pull the loop through, but do not drop the second stitch off the left needle.
• Now, position your left forefinger on the left needle *ahead* of the second stitch.
• Pull gently on the yarn as you transfer the loop to the left needle. Again, do not let the third stitch snuggle up to the second.

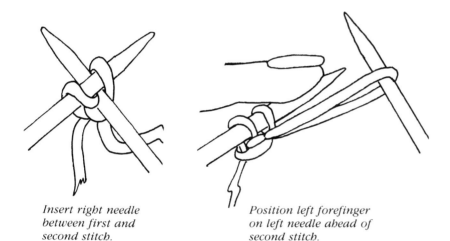
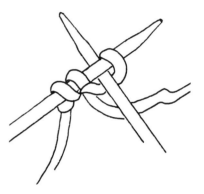

Insert right needle between first and second stitch.

Position left forefinger on left needle ahead of second stitch.

Insert right needle between two previous stitches.

And, it won't if your left forefinger is on the left needle as it should be. This finger acts as a buffer and holds the new stitch away from the previous stitch—a necessary move for tension as well as speed. To pick up a rhythm casting on in this manner, you must be able to insert the right needle quickly *between* the stitches; having to hunt and peck for the opening will not only slow you down, but will result in an uneven tension and a ragged looking selvedge.

4th Stitch on—Continue the third stitch technique, i.e., insert the right needle *between* the two previous stitches on the left needle, and proceed from there.

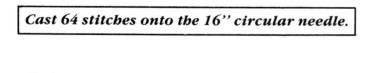

> ***Cast 64 stitches onto the 16" circular needle.***

A word about both:

The 16" needle. This one-piece tool may seem awkward if you are strangers. As you get better acquainted, your hands will adjust to its mold, and you will wonder how you ever managed without its convenience for sleeves, hats, scarves, baby garments, and other small knittings.

The 64 stitches. In the recommended 4-ply knitting worsted weight yarn, this number of stitches should fit comfortably around the needle. However, if this number will not reach from end to end for the first round, or once underway, if you find you must push the stitches around the needle, feel free to add a few more—in multiples of 8. Increase to 72 or 80; that should do it. The more the stitches, the easier they flow around the needle, but the longer it will take to work through the sampler and get on with the sweater.

Imagine for a moment that the stitches you have cast-on are for a sweater. In that case, you have arrived at the first Decision Point. Is the sweater to be a pullover or a cardigan?

Decision Point:

The Pullover—Follow directions for The First Round—Round Knitting.

The Cardigan—Follow directions for The First Row—Flat Knitting. Also see The Cardigan Sweater, p. 151.

The sampler falls into the pullover category. Follow the directions for The First Round—Round Knitting.

The First Round

Round knitting. Round knitting is worked in rounds, and grows toward you. A round is once around the needle from the slip knot stitch around to it again.

METHOD: Transfer the end of the needle with the slip knot stitch to your left hand.
- Untwist and straighten all the stitches on the needle; the bottom of each stitch should head down and be under the needle.
- Hold the end of the needle with the last cast-on stitch and the working yarn in your right hand. (The yarn is on the front of the needle. Pay no attention to it. It should be.)
- Insert the right needle into the slip knot stitch on the left needle, and knit the stitch. This joins your knitting.

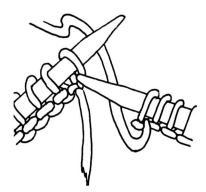

The first stitch—round knitting.

The first row *(for future reference).*

Flat knitting. Flat knitting is worked in rows. A row is once across the needle. Turn your work at the end of every row as on two needles.

METHOD: The end of the needle with the last cast-on stitch and the working yarn remains in your left hand.
- Hold the end of the needle with the slip knot stitch in your right hand.
- Insert the right needle into the last cast-on stitch on the left needle, and knit the stitch. This does not join your knitting. The stitches will untwist and straighten themselves as you work across the row.

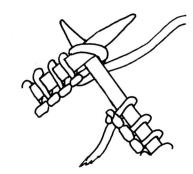

The first stitch—flat knitting.

> **Knit one round.** (The last 2 stitches at the end of the first round are intertwined. Dig them apart; there are two.)

Stop at the end of the first round—before the slip knot stitch. The slip knot loosened when you inserted the right needle to join your work. Tighten it by pushing up on the knot as you pull down on the tail. Don't, by the way, grab the tail and work it in with the next few stitches; this is a habit you must break if you have it. For the tail of the slip knot is crucial to a sweater worked in the round. It identifies the right side seamline of the sweater when the sweater is on. Thus you will know the front from the back as you work. It is the very last end to be tucked in and neatened, for without it a rapid assessment of where you are is not possible.

The term "seamline" is used figuratively as a point of reference to designate either the right or the left side lines of the sweater. The same holds true for the sampler. And, to further identify its right side seamline:

> **Put a marker on the right needle.** Always start and end the rounds at this marker. Slip it from the left needle to the right needle as you work.

Take one last check to be sure the stitches are all straight on the needle. If you do find a twist, correct it now by reversing the last stitch of the round, and taking the yarn through the needle to the back. Beyond this point, it's the start-all-over-again department.

And, yes, in round knitting one round is always ahead of the other. This shift at the seamline is noticeable only if you change color, or are working a pattern. You are the only one who will be aware of it; when the garment is complete, the tiny jog will disappear.

With the first round worked, it's on to Garter Stitch.

Garter Stitch

Garter Stitch produces a weft fabric (one having horizontal tendencies). On a given number of stitches it makes a *wider* fabric than stockinette stitch. Therefore, to be used as a border or a trim on a stockinette stitch garment, it must be narrowed by working it on a smaller needle than that used for the body of the garment, or by reducing the number of stitches by 10%. The surface of a garter stitch fabric is bumpy, and it is reversible.

To count garter stitch rows, each bump is equal to two rows of knitting.

Worked in the flat, it will produce a perfect square if you work twice as many rows as you have stitches on the needle; an interesting idiosyncrasy.

Always start a gauge sample with 6 or 8 rows of garter stitch to prevent the top edge from curling. The sample will then lie flat for the "stitches to the inch" count. Otherwise the job will take three hands; one to hold the top flat, one to hold the gauge measure, and one to count the stitches.

METHOD:
Round. Knit one round, purl one round. Repeat these two rounds.
Flat. Knit every row.

> ***Work 7 rounds of garter stitch.*** You have already knit one round, so start with a purl round.

Stockinette Stitch

Stockinette stitch produces a *warp* fabric (one with vertical tendencies). On a given number of stitches it makes a *narrower* fabric than garter stitch. It is the most common and basic knit fabric. The surface of stockinette stitch is smooth on one side, usually the outside, and bumpy on the other, usually the inside. For design purposes, or simply to get two different looks for the price of one sweater, the fabric can be used inside-out.

METHOD:
Round. Knit every round.
Flat. Knit one row, purl one row. Repeat these two rows.

> ***Work 5 rounds of stockinette stitch.*** As you work, you should feel your sampler pulling in a bit.
>
> ***Knit a few stitches into the 6th round, and break your yarn leaving a 6" tail.*** You may have to cut it if it's a synthetic.

Making Connections

A break can occur in the yarn in any place, at any time, and for a variety of reasons; usually all wrong, inconvenient, and a jolt to one's sense of continuity. Coming to the end of a ball of yarn is final; there is nothing to do but accept it. Not as readily accepted are knots. A great temptation exists to let them slide right by, pretending, or preferring, not to see them. No more. From now on, treat that knot for what it is, a natural break in the yarn, and break it again. You must get rid of the knot. If you are using a commercial yarn, look a few yards ahead of the knot; this is a case of where there is one, there may be two. Then you can rid the yarn of them both at once. Granted you will be wasting the few yards of yarn in between, but this is certainly preferable to another interruption as soon as you are underway again.

Handspinners, early on, become accustomed to knots in their yarn and tend to be more understanding. After all, the tools of the trade are limiting; a bobbin will hold only so much yarn, and there is no alternative. Knots tied with one's own hand are more readily recognized as a temporary connection to be rectified at some future time.

In the case of overly thick or extra thin spots in the yarn, the unintentional ones that are not supposed to be there, you'll have to make your own decision whether to break or not. The circumstance may occur more often with handspun, but commercial yarns are not above having a stray tuft or a twit. Be disciplined, and deal with the imperfection as it comes along. That the flaw is there doesn't mean it should be. Why have a thick spot mar the regularity of your knitting, or worse, a thin spot break in the finished garment? If there is any doubt in your mind, break the yarn.

Changing color or yarn type at a seam line also necessitates breaking the yarn. To add a one-round stripe you might get away with carrying the base yarn up inside your work, but for anything deeper, a clean break is best. Then each end can be eased to tension at the intersection and knotted; this will better control the aforementioned jog at the seam line.

If there is a break in the progression of your knitting, i.e., if you must start anew at a different location in the same piece of work, either in the same color or a contrasting color, treat the new beginning as a change of color.

Now, to get you and your yarn back together again: to connect yarns at a break, follow directions for the particular circumstance, either **Same Color** or **Change of Color.**

Same Color

METHOD:

Round or Flat. Make the connection *near* a side seamline.

Flat knitters. Are you listening? *Never* (*never* except to change color), connect the yarn at the end of a row. Keep that selvedge intact whenever possible. (End of aside to flat knitters.)

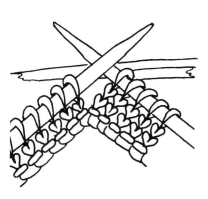

Making connections—same color.

- Work to within 6'' of the end of the old yarn, or leave more if you must to be near a side seam.
- Hold the old yarn parallel to the stitches you have just worked, its end heading right.
- Hold the new yarn parallel to the stitches you are about to work, its end heading left.
- Snatch up both strands of yarn at the stitch you have just worked, and knit, or purl, whatever the case may be, the next two stitches with both strands.
- Drop the old strand and continue working with the new.

On the next round, or row, don't forget you have made a connection. The tails will serve to remind you to work these two "double" stitches as one; else you will wonder from where the extra stitches came. If you are working with a slippery yarn, work three or more stitches with both strands. In the final analysis, these double stitches are undetectable.

Change of Color

METHOD:

Round or Flat. Leaving a 6'' tail, break the old yarn at the right side seamline, or at the end of a row, or wherever you want to change color.

- Insert the right needle into the next stitch to be worked.
- Make a loop with the new yarn 6'' from the end.
- Bring the loop down over the tip of the inserted needle, and pull the yarn through as a stitch. Knot the ends and adjust to tension later.

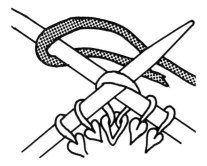

Making connections—change of color.

> *Connect the sampler yarn following directions for Same Color.*
> *Finish knitting the 6th round.*
> *Work 4 more rounds of stockinette stitch.*

The Ribbings

Until now, you may have blithely followed written directions for a ribbing style or, on your own, substituted one for another because you thought it might look better. Looks aside, you must discover how each ribbing acts and feels. The ribbing is the most significant factor in the shaping of a sweater. Your choice of style determines whether the sweater hangs loose, fits snug, or is somewhere in between. As you work the three most common ribbings, one after the other, notice their pull-in tendencies. Then stop, and think. Is that the type of ribbing I want? Will it do the job in this weight yarn? Do I want more or less elasticity? The choice is yours.

Knit One, Purl One

K1, P1 is the least elastic of the ribbings. It is best used with fine yarn for baby wear as shape is not of consequence. It does not have the elasticity to hold in a medium or heavy weight yarn, and will not snap back into shape once stretched. The knit stitches tend to have a crooked appearance no matter how skillfully controlled the tension.

METHOD:
Round. On an even number of stitches, K1, P1, around. Repeat for as many rounds as desired.
Flat. On an uneven number of stitches, repeat these 2 rows:
   • ***Row 1***—K1, P1 across the row, end K1.
   • ***Row 2***—P1, K1 across the row, end P1.

> ***Work 10 rounds of K1, P1.***

Knit One Back, Purl One—the Twisted Rib

Worked correctly, K1b, P1 is a decorative ribbing as the twisted knit stitch gives it a pleasing appearance. Its elasticity factor is practically nil, which explains why Aran Isle sweaters, where it's most often used, simply hang with no shape at all. For a cardigan style, which is more jacket than sweater, this ribbing is fine; but if you'd rather your pullover had a bit more pull-in, see K2, P2.

K1b, P1 is a tricky rib, and method must change to work it in the round. Otherwise, the ribbing on a round hat won't match the ribbing on its companion flat mittens. You may have discovered this peculiarity already. Have you ever worked a sweater in the flat, and then worked its neck ribbing in the round? If you have, note the difference of the knit stitches. In the neck ribbing, they are tense; in the body and sleeve ribbings, they are at ease. The reason for this dissimilarity is that in flat knitting the K1b stitch of the outside row is purled on the inside row, and thus has a chance to straighten up. In round knitting, the K1b stitch is twisted every round. Who can blame it for becoming stiff, tight, and slanted? It is being strangled.

Therefore, in round knitting, to obtain the same soft, relaxed decorative twist as in flat knitting, you must alternate a round of K1b, P1, with a round of plain K1, P1. To keep track of these alternating rounds, it might be wise to put a second marker on the needle at the seamline as you start the K1b, P1 round, and remove it as you start the plain K1, P1 round. Then if the phone rings, or the paper boy knocks, you will know where you are when you return—rather a one, if by land; two, if by sea, sort of reminder.

K1b: With the tip of the right needle heading left, insert it out through the back of the knit stitch, and complete the stitch as usual. This gives a twist to the knit stitch.

METHOD:
Round. On an even number of stitches, alternate these two rounds:
> **Round 1**—K1b, P1 around.
> **Round 2**—K1, P1 around.

Flat. On an uneven number of stitches, repeat these 2 rows:
> **Row 1**—K1b, P1 across the row, end K1b.
> **Row 2**—P1, K1b across the row, end P1.

> ┌─────────────────────────────────────┐
> │ **Work 10 rounds of twisted rib.** │
> └─────────────────────────────────────┘

The K1b stitch for twisted rib.

Knit Two, Purl Two

K2, P2 is a good, snug all purpose rib for use with any weight yarn. Be generous: the more of it you do, the more elasticity it will have. Work at least 2'', if not 3'', on the body of a sweater; 3'' to 4'' on a sleeve cuff, especially for the small set. If the ribbing does stretch out of shape, a good washing, or, if time is short, a good lengthwise tug, will snap it right back to its former state; you can't destroy it.

And, to give more shape to that Aran Isle pullover, work a round of K2b, P2 alternately with a round of plain K2, P2—a ribbing that retains the decorative twist, but with more pull-in.

METHOD:
Round. On a number of stitches divisible by 4, K2, P2 around. Repeat for as many rounds as desired.
Flat. On a number of stitches divisible by 4, plus 2, repeat these 2 rows:
> **Row 1**—K2, P2 across the row, end K2.
> **Row 2**—P2, K2 across the row, end P2.

> ## *Work 8 rounds of K2, P2.*

Did you feel that knitted fabric pulling in? What a difference a stitch makes; K2, P2 hardly seems related to K1, P1. And that statement is the key to the elasticity of ribbings. The higher the number of *equal* alternating knits and purls, the greater the amount of pull-in to the fabric. If you thought K2, P2 was an improvement over K1, P1, try some K3, P3. The Scottish fishermen's "ganseys" were all ribbed with K3, P3. For looks? No, for the purposeful, hug-the-body qualities of this ribbing. The last thing these hard-working salts needed was a loose sweater flopping about as they struggled with their catch. And, to avoid chafed wrists, the gansey sleeves were three-quarter length. Oh, were they smart. Why push up a wet, soggy sleeve when a shorter one is the cure?

So, if you want a very snug ribbing, use K3, P3. Just remember it must be worked over a number of stitches divisible by 6 in the round, and a number of stitches divisible by 6, plus 3 in the flat. And, on it goes—K4, P4; to K5, P5; to K6, P6—each with a greater amount of snap and bounce than the one before. Sometime, and you may put the sampler aside to try it now if you wish, heed the advice of Mary Thomas* and work the following two fabric samples. Not only will you see how alive K4, P4 is, but you will clearly see how the choice of a pattern stitch will change the width and the height of a knitted fabric.

Sampler A—Ribbed Fabric
METHOD: Use 2 double-pointed needles.
Cast on 32 stitches.
• Work K4, P4 for 40 rows. Cast off.

Sampler B—Welt Fabric
METHOD: Use 2 double-pointed needles.
Cast on 32 stitches.
Row 1—Purl.
Row 2—Knit.
Row 3—Purl.
Row 4—Knit.
Row 5—Knit.
Row 6—Purl.
Row 7—Knit.
Row 8—Purl.
• Repeat these 8 rows 5 times for a total of 40 rows. Cast-off.

*Mary Thomas, *Mary Thomas's Book of Knitting Patterns,* p. 17.

Incredible? Do you see why a sweater in a ribbing pattern fits like a second skin? Can you also see why a sweater in a Garter Stitch Rib pattern would not?

Garter Stitch Rib:
> **Round 1**—K4, P4 (or whatever the number), around.
> **Round 2**—Knit.

The all-knit round counteracts the rib round. The result is a sweater that looks like, but does not act like, a rib.

It's not on the agenda, but by all means try one, some, or all of these other ribbings in the sampler.

Then, it's on to add a bit of color.

Stripes in Ribbing

For a neat, clean-cut stripe in a ribbing, an all-knit round, or row, must be worked on the outside of the fabric to introduce the new color. This all-knit round, or row, prevents the new color from dropping below the old color in the purl stitches. The interplay of colors then borders the stripe on the inside. Keep this phenomenon in mind if you intend to roll up a sleeve cuff or the brim of a cap. On the other hand, if you intend to keep it rolled up forever, and if you are working in the flat, reverse the procedure and work an all-purl row on the outside. Remember to make use of this technique whenever there is a purl stitch involved in a color change; don't restrict its use to ribbings per se. All-over sweater patterns, such as K6, P2, or P7, K1, are variations of ribbing patterns, and their stripes should be treated in the same manner.

METHOD: *(round or flat)* With the new color, and on the outside of the fabric, **knit every stitch** around the round or across the row. In other words, forget momentarily that you are working a ribbing pattern. On the next round, or row, resume the ribbing pattern. Continue ribbing in the new color for the desired depth of the stripe.

To return to the original color, or to change to still another, repeat the all knit round or row on the outside.

> *Work a 4 round stripe in the K2, P2 ribbing.*
> *Work 8 rounds of K2, P2.* Take a peek inside; design possibilities?
> *Work 3 rounds of stockinette stitch, adding a marker after the 32nd stitch.*

The sampler now has two side "seams." The marker at the tail is the right seamline. The marker you have just added is the left seamline.

Short Rows*

Short rows add extra length to the back of a sweater, a detail that allows a custom fit for those who are always tugging down the back of their sweater. Working the technique once adds *two* rounds or rows to the back, and for this reason, once is generally enough. Consider the diameter of your yarn, and consequently, your number of rows to the inch, a measure you can usually ignore. In a medium to heavyweight yarn, two rounds or rows could add 1/2", or more: an ample amount. In a fine yarn four extra rounds or rows may be needed. In any case, work the short rows about 3" above the ribbing, and again 3" above that if a second set is applicable.

If short rows are added, put a large safety pin somewhere in the back of the sweater as a reminder. You don't want the short rows ending up in the front.

Short rows do have their limitations. Confine them to a plain sweater, or one in which the extra rows will not interfere with a pattern.

The directions for working short rows are the same for both round and flat, except for the last step. For the sampler, be sure to follow the *round* directions at that point.

METHOD: *(round or flat)* Work around (or across) to within 3 stitches of the left seam line.
- Put the yarn forward (as if to purl), slip 1 stitch as if to purl, put the yarn back, put the slipped stitch back on the left needle.
- *Turn your work.* (You are now looking down into the sampler, or if this were a sweater in the round, the sweater.)
- Purl across to within 3 stitches of the right seamline, put the yarn back (as if to knit), slip 1 stitch as if to purl, put the yarn forward, put the slipped stitch back on the left needle.
- *Turn your work.* You have wrapped the yarn around 1 stitch at each turn to avoid a hole in the fabric. The wrapping is in a horizontal position. Now, to stand it up:
- Work across to within 3 stitches of the left seamline. *With the tip of the right needle lift the front of the wrapping and put it on the left needle with the stitch it was wrapped around. Knit the two together as 1 stitch.*
- *Round only.* Continue working around to the 3rd stitch after the right seamline. Repeat * to *. All done. Finish the round.
- *Flat only.* Continue working to the end of the row. On the next row, work to within 3 stitches of the right seamline. Repeat * to *, except purl the two together as 1 stitch. All done. Finish the row.

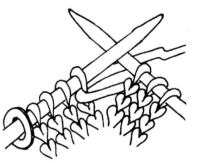

Short rows—the wrapping

*Elizabeth Zimmermann, *Knitter's Almanac,* p. 147.

> *Work the Short Rows once.*
> *Work 2 rounds of stockinette stitch.*
> *Stop at the right seam line.*
> *Remove the marker.* For a short while you will be working back and forth on the circular needle—flat knitting.
> *Read Chain Selvedge, then move on to Cardigan Border.*

Chain Selvedge

A neat selvedge is essential to the front edges of a cardigan sweater, and the sides of a sweatshirt pocket. For that matter, it is essential to anything knit in the flat. Pity the knitters of sweaters in pieces who attempt to sew an even seam without the consistency of even selvedges. This pity extends back a few pages to include those who connect their yarns at the end of the row. It might be possible to hide an irregular selvedge in a seam, but it's not an enviable job.

By slipping the first stitch of every row, as if to purl, you will be rewarded with a uniform edge—the chain selvedge. Practice this slip 1 move until it becomes second nature whenever you are working in the flat. Pay particular attention to the position of the yarn, for though you are slipping as if to purl the yarn is not always in the front. If a chosen pattern doesn't have an extra stitch to slip, add one; a simple solution, a world of difference, and vital if the edge is to be exposed to the naked eye.

METHOD:

Flat. In flat knitting, always slip the first stitch as if to purl. This refers only to the position of the needles. The position of the yarn varies from front to back:

• If the first stitch was knitted at the end of the previous row, slip as if to purl with the yarn in *front*.

• If the first stitch was purled at the end of the previous row, slip as if to purl with the yarn in *back*.

The slip 1 selvedge resembles a chain of stitches, each chain stitch being equal to two rows of knitting. Because of its appearance and ratio, the chain of stitches clears up a sometimes perplexing chore for all knitters, that is, knitting up the stitches for the neck ribbing of a sweater. Even a sweater worked in the round must be worked back and forth on the needle once the neck shaping starts, but by slipping the first stitch of every row, you will be rewarded with a visible chain of stitches. No longer will you have to wonder what, where, or how many to knit up; they will be right there looking at you. The added bonus is that the proportion will be correct, and the neck ribbing will lie flat. Jumping ahead a bit, but while on the subject—

Knitting Into the Chain Selvedge.

METHOD: Hold the edge of the fabric horizontally in your left hand so that the edge is up straight and the chain doesn't roll to the back.
- Put the tip of the right needle under both strands of the chain stitch, take the yarn around as if to knit, and pull the loop through onto the needle.
- Repeat for the length of the chain.

Knitting into the chain selvedge.

The Cardigan Border

The Cardigan Border is a 6 stitch border of K1, P1. It is worked at each end of the needle right along with the body of the sweater. The K1, P1 rib makes an edge sturdy enough to support a button; its heftiness is more visible inside than out. The obvious advantage to a knit-along border is that once the sweater is done, it's done; there are no strange additions to be made. In a medium-to-heavy weight yarn, a 6 stitch border should be wide enough. However, in a fine yarn you may want to increase to 8 or 10 stitches in K1, P1. If that sounds like too many, remember the purl stitches hide, so the actual border is only half that width. For some reason, the K1, P1 acts more like it should in a border than in an all-around ribbing. Garter and seed stitch borders, though perhaps more decorative, lack stability. Confine them to your afghans and scarves.

The Cardigan Border in the sampler will be worked on a mini version of a placket neck opening. To prepare for this, turn the sampler so that you are looking down into it. The stitch with the working yarn should be in your left hand. Insert the right needle between the first two stitches on the left needle, and proceed to:

Cast on 6 stitches.
Purl the 6 cast-on stitches and all the others around to the opening you have created. (Do not slip the first one, as it is not yet an established stitch.)
Turn your work.

You are now in a position to work the cardigan border over the first and last 6 stitches on the needle. You will be working back and forth on the needle—flat knitting. Keep the stitches in between the borders in stockinette stitch. To do so means that you will knit these stitches on the outside rows, but they must be purled on the inside row. If this were a sweater with a pattern stitch in between the borders, it might very well have to have its knits and purls reversed for the inside row. Hence, the word *work* in the phrase, *work* across to the last 6 stitches. It means to do whatever you must do to keep your pattern in order.

And, one final caution—carefully watch the position of the yarn for the slip stitch at the beginning of each row. Notice also that the slip stitch takes the place of what should be a K1 at the beginning of Row 1—The Outside Row, and what should be a P1 at the beginning of Row 2—The Inside Row.

METHOD:
Row 1—The Outside Row. Slip 1 (slip as if to purl with the yarn in *back,* bring the yarn to the front), P1, K1, P1, K1, P1, work across to the last 6 stitches, P1, K1, P1, K1, P1, K1. ***Turn your work.***
Row 2—The Inside Row. Slip 1 (slip as if to purl with the yarn in *front,* bring the yarn to the back), K1, P1, K1, P1, K1, work across to the last 6 stitches, K1, P1, K1, P1, K1, P1. ***Turn your work.***
• Repeat rows 1 and 2 for the length of the border.

> ***Work 4 rows with Cardigan Border.***

Buttonholes

Of all the methods that exist for making buttonholes, there is only one that will do the job swiftly and neatly: the Yarn Over, or YO for short. This quick maneuver, followed by an equally quick Knit Two Together, or K2tog., for short, guarantees a proper buttonhole as the size of the hole changes with the weight of the yarn. The opening is therefore proportionate for an appropriate button.
LARGE BUTTONS are distracting. So are LARGE BUTTONHOLES. How sad to see those sweaters, particularly Aran Isles; a row of great wooden buttons marching up one side front, paired with a row of misshaped holes marching down the other. Weeks, perhaps months, of knitting vanish before your very eyes. Do away with these offenders. Use proper size buttons color-matched to the yarn, and replace those complex slots with a simple YO. Then, all your beautiful knitting will be the focal point.

Now, how do you space the buttonholes? To begin with, put two in the ribbing, the area that takes the most stress and strain. Make one about 1/2" after you start, and the other about 1/2" before you stop. When buttoned, the two will equalize the pressure and hold the bottom closing straight—no gap. Space the rest about 3" apart, or use another sweater for a guide. These little fellows hide in the purl groove; if one does end up in the wrong spot, stitch him together—no one will know.

An alternative to the button dilemma is to eliminate the embellishment entirely. Work buttonholes at each end of the needle, and with a coordinating or contrasting knitted cord, tie the sweater as a shoe. This option admittedly changes the nature of the garment from cardigan to pullover—unless you have the time and patience to lace and unlace for each wearing. Nevertheless, the idea has merit; kept laced, the sweater has a chance of being worn. How many cardigans are? They are thrown over the shoulders, draped around the neck, or tied at the waist and sat on; a shawl or a blanket would be more practical and present a better picture. No wonder that nine times out of ten, the sweater that stands out in a crowd is a pullover. Displayed on the body proper, as intended, it makes a positive statement, and thus attracts attention. At the same time, it reflects its wearer's positive qualities; not the type to hem and haw, this one—do I need a sweater, or don't I? A decision was made, the sweater pulled on, and worn out the door to catch eyes.

METHOD: To make a buttonhole, substitute the following beginning or ending for the beginning or ending of Row 1 of Cardigan Border:

> ***Women:*** Begin Row 1—Slip 1, P1, K1, YO*, K2tog., P1.
> ***Men:***   End Row 1—P1, K1, YO*, K2tog., P1, K1.

*To a right hand knitter, YO simply means to put the yarn forward as if to purl. The yarn then goes over the needle by itself from this position as you knit the next two stitches together, thus adding one stitch to compensate for the one you are losing by knitting two together. On the next row, work the YO stitch as K1.

The buttonhole—YO, K2tog.

> ***Work a buttonhole row.*** (Women: Begin Row 1).
> ***Work 2 more rows of Cardigan Border.*** (All this seemingly blank knitting in between the borders will be the home for pockets.)

> ***At the beginning of the next row, cast off* the 6 added stitches, then purl across to the last 6 stitches, and work the border.***
>   **To cast-off: Slip 1, K1, pass the slip stitch over the knit; P1, pass the knit over the purl; K1, pass the purl over the knit; etc.*
> ***At the beginning of the next row, work the border, and then knit to the end.***
> ***Rejoin the sampler*** *by inserting the right needle (the one with the working yarn) into the first stitch on the left needle.*
> ***Knit one round.***
> ***Put a marker back on the needle at the right seamline.*** *Check to be sure the left seamline marker is still there.*

A placket neck in a sweater would, of course, not be joined back together, but worked straight and open to the top. By joining your work you have created a side placket, or if it were in the front, a fly? Sew a button on the flap under the buttonhole to keep it closed and out of your way.

The Sweatshirt Pocket

This pocket certainly needs no introduction. It's always right there with you, ready to warm your hands in an instant: a built-in muff, if you will. And, this one is truly built-in, or rather knit-in, without a single stitch to sew. Though the concept is not new to you, the construction might be: the pocket grows out of the ribbing and then joins forces with the sweater in progress. The principle of its construction remains the same for any size sweater.

The sweatshirt pocket in the sampler is a mini version of one in the sweater on page 141. To construct a sweatshirt pocket in a sweater, the number of stitches will not be the same. Refer to The Sweatshirt Pocket on page 175.

> ***Work the following directions line by line for the sampler only.***

METHOD: The front of the sampler has 32 stitches. The pocket will cover the center 12.
- Starting at the right seamline, work 10 stitches beyond the ***left*** seamline.
- ***Stop.***
- With your finger trace the 11th stitch down to its source in the row above the ribbing.

- Slide a fine double-pointed needle under one half of this 11th stitch. Each stitch has two sides. It doesn't matter which one.
- Aiming to the left, slide the fine needle under one-half of each of the next 11 stitches. You should have 12 "stitches" on the fine double-pointed needle.

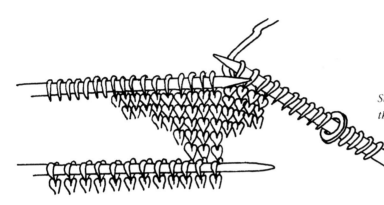

Slide the fine needle under one-half of each of the next 11 stitches.

- Connect a *new* yarn at the first stitch on the right end of the fine needle. *Do not* break the working yarn of the sampler itself. You will need it right where it is in a minute. Use the other end of the sampler yarn, or better yet, a scrap of a contrasting color.
- Using a sampler size (or close to it), double-pointed needle, knit the 12 stitches from the fine needle. Put the fine needle aside; it has done its job—which was to pick up this bottom row of stitches without stretching them any more than necessary. The flap that is to be the pocket is worked on two sampler-size double-pointed needles—flat knitting.

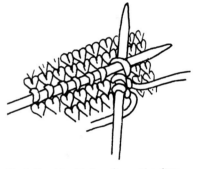

Knit the 12 stitches from the fine needle.

- **Turn your work,** and purl the 12 stitches. You will now be working back and forth on the 12 stitches, knitting a row, purling a row. To practice chain selvedge:
    Knit rows—slip the first stitch as if to purl, yarn in back.
    Purl rows—slip the first stitch as if to purl, yarn in front.
- Work until the pocket knitting reaches the sampler knitting.
- **Stop** after a purl row.
- Break the pocket yarn, and secure it.
- Hold the 12 stitches on the pocket needle in front of the next 12 stitches to be knit on the sampler needle.
- With the sampler yarn and needle, join the pocket to the sampler by knitting together a stitch from the pocket needle with a stitch from the sampler needle.
- **Finish the knit round.**

Knit together a stitch from the flap with a stitch from the sweater.

Did you survive? Do you have a pocket? Wasn't it easy? This Rube Goldberg creation is the result of being too lazy to get up and search the books for a sweater with a pocket, and then wade through directions to discover how others have tackled the job. This piece of ingenuity seemed logical, and the end product is a success.

Important: In a sweater, work the first and last 6 stitches in Cardigan Border for a firm edge on each side of the pocket. In the sampler you only had 12 stitches to begin with so, oh well, you can figure that one out. Notice the curl to the stockinette stitch edge—worked to be sewn, it would be fine; but for an edge to be on view, it doesn't pass muster. Nor would it wear; it's too flimsy. The Cardigan Border provides the sturdiness needed on the edges.

For future reference: If for some other flat project a 6 stitch border is too wide, work just the second and next to last stitch as a purl on the knit row. This purl stitch will keep the edge flat.

The Bar Increase

Though there are many styles of increases, the bar increase is used to shape the body and the sleeves of the basic sweater. This increase is worked in two ways, either evenly-spaced, or in pairs. It is worked evenly-spaced to increase the number of stitches from the body and sleeve ribbing to the body and sleeve proper. It is worked in pairs to gradually shape the sleeves.

The bar increase produces a visible, horizontal bump, or bar, to the left of the original stitch. Worked evenly-spaced in the last round of ribbing, these bumps mingle nicely with the purl stitches. Worked in pairs in a sleeve, the bumps form a pattern, or track, at the seamline and can easily be counted.

In the sampler, the bar increase is worked in pairs to somewhat simulate the sleeve seamline possibilities.

METHOD: Knit the stitch, do not drop the stitch off the left needle, knit out through the back of the same stitch, and then drop the stitch off the left needle.

Knit the next stitch, do not drop the stitch off the needle.

Knit out through the back of the same stitch.

Then, drop the stitch off the needle.

Evenly-Spaced

In a sweater, evenly-spaced increases are worked in the last round, or row, of the body and/or the sleeve ribbing while you are still on the ribbing size needle. Keep the round, or row, in your ribbing pattern, except for the stitch you increase; work the bar increase into that stitch whether it be a knit or a purl. To work a purl increase into a purl stitch will leave a hole.

METHOD: To increase evenly-spaced throughout a round, or across a row: divide the number of stitches on the needle by the number of stitches you must increase. The quotient is the stitch in which to work the bar increase.

Example: If you have 56 stitches on the needle, and you must increase 8 stitches, divide 56 by 8. The quotient is 7. Therefore, work the bar increase into every 7th stitch throughout the round, or across the row. In round knitting, start counting at the seamline marker. In flat knitting start counting at the beginning of the row, unless you are working a border. In that case, space the increases between the border stitches.

The division does not always come out even, of course. If it doesn't, don't worry about it. Increase into the quotient stitch, but not into any part of the remainder. The remainder takes care of itself.

In Pairs

To shape the fitted sleeve and the semi sleeve, a pair of bar increases are worked at the seamline with 0, 1, or 2 stitches between them. As the bar of the bar increase is always to the left of the original stitch, it will look as if there is an additional stitch for separation. The seamlines, A, or B, or C differ only in their width. In the sampler, you will work all three simultaneously. In a sleeve, select *one* of the three and work *it* at the seamline.

METHOD: To increase in pairs, use A, B, or C:

> *Increase A*—Knit to within 1 stitch of the seamline marker, *increase,* slip marker, *increase.*

> *Increase B*—Knit to within 1 stitch of the seamline marker, *increase,* slip marker, K1, *increase.*

> *Increase C*—Knit to within 2 stitches of the seamline marker, *increase,* K1, slip marker, K1, *increase.*

To prepare the sampler:

> ***Knit one round, removing the marker at the left seamline. Knit one round putting markers after the 20th, 40th, and 60th stitches.*** Note: it will be easier to work these make-believe seamlines if the markers are of different colors and differ too from the one at the right seamline. Mark the book as to which increase will be worked at what marker color. Then you can talk and knit at the same time without losing track of where you are.

In a sleeve, the pair of increases are worked about every inch as you work its length. To save time here in the sampler, the increases are worked every other round. Therefore, the track will not look exactly as it does in the sweater. If you happen to prefer another style increase, work it instead of the bar increase, or work them side by side for comparison.

> ***Knit 1 round, working:***
> Increase A at first marker, _____ (marker color),
> Increase B at second marker, _____ (marker color),
> Increase C at third marker, _____ (marker color).
> ***Knit 1 straight round.***
> ***Repeat these 2 rounds, three times.*** On the last round, remove all the markers except the one at the right seamline.
> You now have 88 stitches on the needle.

Stripes

What's your pleasure? How do you see them? Are they bold and bright, or mellow and subdued; single round statements, or an all-over thesis; flat and smooth, or full of texture. From the earliest of times, individuals have personalized their fabrics in this most elementary manner. And, like the proverbial duck takes to water, sweaters take to stripes. Scraps would be scraps without them.

The Knit Stripe

There are so many variables, but for the average size 40 sweater a single round stripe will take about 3 to 5 yards of yarn. If you are using scraps and want a more accurate measure, try this: Stop at the seamline a few rounds before the stripe. Pull out 5 yards of your working yarn—you don't need a yard stick, just nose to fingertip—and tie a knot at the end of this measure. Start at the seamline and work one round. How far are you from the knot?

METHOD: *(round or flat).* At the beginning of a round, or an outside row, and with another color, or with another yarn, knit every stitch around the round or across the row.

Continue in stockinette stitch for the desired depth. To return to the original yarn, or make another change, repeat the above.

The Purl Stripe

Hark back to stripes in ribbing and remember what happens with a change of color, or yarn, when there is a purl stitch involved. The same holds true in a stockinette stitch fabric. For what looks like a simple purl stripe, isn't. A round or row of knit must be worked in the stripe yarn first. This round or row of knit stitches disappears under the next round or row of purl stitches, thus making a clear purl stripe. The humble purl, in another color or another yarn, produces a proud stripe. You must figure on double the amount of yarn for a "single" purl stripe.

METHOD:

Round. Knit 1 round with another color, or another yarn.
Purl 1 round with the same.
Continue working purl rounds for the desired stripe depth.
To return to the original yarn, knit the next round.

Flat. Starting on the outside:
Knit 2 rows with another color, or another yarn.
To continue, purl the outside rows, and knit the inside rows for the desired stripe depth.
To return to the original yarn, knit it in on the outside, or purl it in on the inside.

> ***Work a one round knit stripe.***
> ***Knit three rounds with the sampler yarn.***
> ***Work a "one round" (actually two rounds— see above) purl stripe.***
> ***Knit three rounds with the sampler yarn.***

The Raised Stripe

Weavers, move over. You no longer have a corner on the market for texture—the raised stripe is the knitter's answer to your soumak and twining. The yarn loops along above the fabric, the more contrast to the background the better. A perfect haven for odd lengths of lumpy handspun or other novelty yarns. Yet don't discount working this stripe in the selfsame yarn, for it offers a subtle swag in relief, tone on tone, to decorate an otherwise plain fabric.

To achieve that subtle swag, you must work Rounds or Rows 1 *and* 2. To produce a linked chain of texture, work all 4 rounds or rows. It is understood that you are working these rounds or rows in the same yarn, or another color, or another yarn.

METHOD:

Round. On an even number of stitches:

> **Round 1**—Slip 1 (as if to purl, yarn in back), K1, around.
>
> **Round 2**—Slip 1 (as if to purl, yarn in front), P1, around.
>
> **Round 3**—K1, slip 1 (as if to purl, yarn in back), around.
>
> **Round 4**—P1, slip 1 (as if to purl, yarn in front), around.

Flat. On an uneven number of stitches:

> **Row 1**—*Slip 1 (as if to purl, yarn in back), K1*.
> Repeat * to * across the row, ending slip 1.
>
> **Row 2**—Repeat Row 1.
>
> **Row 3**—*K1, slip 1 (as if to purl, yarn in back) *.
> Repeat * to * across the row, ending K1.
>
> **Row 4**—Repeat Row 3.

Try the Raised Stripe in your sampler this way:

> *Work rounds 1 and 2 in another color.*
> *Knit 2 rounds with the sampler yarn.*
> *Work rounds 1, 2, 3, and 4 in another color.*
> *Knit 2 rounds with the sampler yarn.*

That gives you the idea of first, the swag, and then, the chain. By all means, experiment in the sampler with different yarns and colors if you want.

The Raglan Seamline Decreases

To shape the yoke of the basic sweater and all its variations, you must decrease at the four raglan seamlines. Offered here are six different methods of working the seamlines. Your choice depends on the style of the sweater, fancy or casual; the yarn of the sweater, smooth or textured; and the design of the sweater, plain or patterned. Each method has its own characteristics and appearance, and the seamlines vary being two, three, or four stitches wide. Think of each seamline as a whole; the sum of its parts.

Each seamline is constructed with a combination of decreases, one worked before the seamline marker, and one worked after the seamline marker with 0, 1, or 2 knit stitches in between. The first four seamlines are worked using K2tog. in combination with SSK.

Decrease—K2tog.

K2tog.—Insert the right needle into the front of 2 stitches and knit them together as if they were one. **K2tog. leans right.**

SSK—Slip as if to **knit,** slip as if to **knit,** insert the left needle into the front of the two stitches (from left to right), and knit them together as if they were one. **SSK leans left.**

Raglan Seamlines A, B, B-Reverse and C

Method: (round or flat) The seamlines are worked on the outside of the sweater.

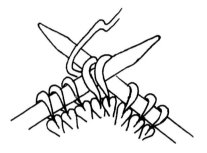

Decrease—SSK.

> **Seamline A**—Knit to within 2 stitches of the seamline marker, *K2tog.,* slip marker, *SSK.*
>
> **Seamline B**—Knit to within 2 stitches of the seamline marker,· *K2tog.,* slip marker, K1, *SSK.*
>
> **Seamline B-Reverse**—Knit to within 2 stitches of the seamline marker, *SSK,* slip marker, K1, *K2tog.*
>
> **Seamline C**—Knit to within 3 stitches of the seamline marker, *K2tog.,* K1, slip marker, K1, *SSK.*

Their Characteristics:

> **Seamline A**—"comes together" as a *perforation.* Use it whenever you do not want a seamline interfering with a pattern. This two-stitch seamline hides, and in a textured yarn, it disappears altogether. However, in a plain stockinette stitch yoke, the fact that SSK does not exactly match K2tog. is evident. This discrepancy points up the problem with decreasing in pairs—nothing exactly matches K2tog. But, in the completed garment, the focus is on the seamline as a whole, and this fact is not of primary importance. The seamline is presentable.
>
> **Seamline B**—is a three stitch wide *raised* seamline. Give it a tug after a few rounds to shape it up. This is the best all-purpose seamline, and it is suitable for any weight yarn.
>
> **Seamline B-Reverse**—is *flat* with one center knit stitch visible. B-Reverse makes a daintier seamline than B, and is suitable for a light weight yarn. It is so named B-Reverse, as the SSK decrease is worked before the marker, and the K2tog. after the marker—just the opposite of B.
>
> **Seamline C**—is a wider version of B. As a four stitch raised seamline, its use is best confined to a sweater for a broad shouldered individual.

Seamline A

Seamline B

Seamline B-Reverse

Seamline C

Seamline D

Seamline E

For a sweater, select *one* of the four, and use *it* at each seam-line. In the sampler, you will try all four in one round, so as with increases, again devise a color code with your markers.

To prepare the sampler:

> **Knit one round putting markers after the 22nd, 44th, and 66th stitches.** Use the right seam-line marker for the fourth seamline.
>
> As you work the seamlines, pay particular attention to the position of *K2tog.* and *SSK* as regards the markers.
>
> **Knit 1 round working:**
> Seamline A at first marker, _____ (marker color).
> Seamline B at second marker, _____ (marker color).
> Seamline B-Rev. at third marker, ____ (marker color).
> Seamline C at fourth marker, _____ (marker color).
>
> **Knit 1 round straight.**
>
> **Repeat the 2 rounds, three times.** On the last round remove all the markers except the one at the right seamline.

The raglan seamline in the sweater has a halting beginning, as you will be working a decrease round every 4th round, or row, three times. But once underway, you will be working a decrease round, or row, every other round as you did in the sampler. There-fore, the seamlines in the sweater will eventually look as they do in the sampler.

Individually, give the four seamlines a lengthwise tug to shape them up, and compare their appearance to the preceding descrip-tions. If you want, hang a small tag on each for quick reference.

Raglan Seamlines D and E

In a plain stockinette stitch sweater, a little more detail at the raglan seamline might be in order as this could be the sweater's only discernable feature. Though not included in the sampler itself, try Seamlines D and E at your leisure, and keep their characteristics in mind for just such an opportunity. Seamlines D and E are con-structed with a combination of the decreases PSSO and PSSO-R.

> **PSSO**—Slip 1 stitch as if to purl, knit 1 stitch, insert the left needle into the front of the slipped stitch, and pass the slip stitch over the knit stitch, dropping it off the left needle. **PSSO leans left.**

PSSO-R—Knit one stitch. Put it back on the left needle. Insert the tip of the right needle as if to purl into the stitch to the left of the returned stitch and pass it over the returned stitch and drop it off the right needle. Slip the resulting stitch back on the right needle. **PSSO-R leans right.**

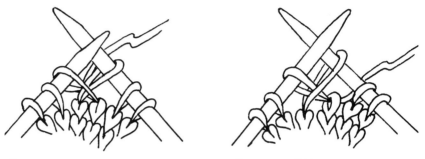

Decrease—PSSO   Decrease—PSSO-R

METHOD: *(round or flat)* The seamlines are worked on the outside of the sweater.

Seamline D—Knit to within 2 stitches of the marker, *PSSO,* slip marker, *PSSO-R.*

Seamline E—Knit to within 2 stitches of the marker, *PSSO,* slip marker, K1, *PSSO-R.*

Their characteristics:

Seamline D—results in a *feather stitch* seamline. Use it as an alternative to A for a two-stitch seamline. The decreases match heading in the opposite directions, and its feathery appearance dresses up the yoke.

Seamline E—is a wider version of D with the *feather stitches more pronounced,* as they are separated by a knit stitch. This seamline is quite prominent: in a plain sweater, it is fine; in a patterned or striped sweater, it could be distracting.

Decreases—evenly spaced *(for future reference)*

Though decreases are not used evenly-spaced in the construction of the sweater itself, they are here for the record if you decide on a hem at the neck.

METHOD: To decrease stitches evenly spaced across a row, or in a round:
- Divide the number of stitches on the needle by the number of stitches you must decrease.
- Knit the quotient figure together with the stitch before it.

Example: If you have 64 stitches on the needle, and you must decrease 8 stitches, divide 64 by 8. The quotient figure is 8. Therefore, knit the 7th and 8th stitches together across the row or in the round.

Again, don't worry about the remainder if your division doesn't come out even.

Now, to be ready for Two Color Knitting, you must have a number of stitches divisible by 8 to work the pattern; you have 56, which is. However, on a 16'' needle, more is better. So, turn back to Increases—Evenly Spaced, and:

> **Knit 1 round, increasing 8 stitches.**

Two Color Knitting

Two color knitting is as ancient to the knitted fabric as striping; it was another means of incorporating a refreshing note of a second color, or more, into a garment, while, no doubt, enlivening a knitter's daily chore. For knitting, as well as all the prior steps leading to the creation of the yarn itself, was on some family member's list—a necessary task, unheard of as a "hobby". What better way to make the job more stimulating and the garment more cheerful than to work with two colors?

Perhaps issue could be taken with the descriptive term, two-color knitting, for a fabric striped with a color is in effect two color knitting. What the phrase implies, and does not say, is that the two colors are worked *at the same time* in one round. Those who describe the process as double-knitting are more on the mark, for the resulting fabric is layered—one strand of yarn behind the other. This fact offers the third and most plausible explanation for the existence of two color knitting—warmth.

A word to the handspinners among you—don't be hesitant to use unevenly spun and/or dyed yarns for two color knitting. Though your handspun may not produce the distinct color sequence typical of today's smooth commercial yarn, the resulting design will have a soft, mysterious beauty of its own, the look of its past. The only dissuading factor is that after all that spinning and dyeing, half of the handspun will be hidden from view.

Two color knitting is neater and less complicated if worked in the round and executed with two hands, one color in each. This allows you to concentrate on the outside of the fabric, while the yarn behaves itself on the inside. You may not become an accomplished knitter with the "other" hand, but you can certainly manage the technique for a few rounds to add a color design to a sweater.

There are two basic types of knitters—so called right hand (English), and left hand (Continental)—and a myriad of variations of each. In both types, the right hand controls the mechanics of making the stitch. It is the hand that holds the yarn and controls the tension that designates whether one is a right or left hand knitter— a right hand knitter holds the yarn in the right hand, a left hand knitter holds the yarn in the left. The choice of style is not based on "being" right or left handed. Many right handed individuals knit the left hand style. However, most left handed individuals find left hand knitting more to their liking.

Left hand knitting is much quicker, as a whole step is eliminated in the process of making a stitch. To a right hand knitter, this may seem like cheating; yet, there on the needle is a perfect stitch with one-third the effort.

METHOD:
To knit a right hand stitch:
• Put the right needle in.
• Put the right yarn around.
• Pull the right yarn through.

Put the right needle in.

Put the yarn around.

Pull the right yarn through.

To knit a left hand stitch:
• Put the right needle in.
• Pull the left yarn through.

A left hand stitch.

Now, try a practice round:

Place the ball of yarn you are using on your right side, with the yarn over the right forefinger. Place a ball of contrasting yarn on your left side, with the yarn over the left forefinger.

> **Alternate a right hand stitch with a left hand stitch starting at the right seamline marker and working around to it again. Work 2 rounds of stockinette stitch with your original color.**

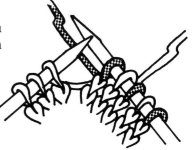

Two-color knitting—yarn position.

A simple practice round yet effective in its own right. These little heart shaped stitches would brighten any sweater, quickly and easily. Imagine that round worked in the flat, both colors in one hand, and the tedious crossing of yarns for each stitch; there is no comparison. Designs with as many as 4 or 5 stitches of one color in a series can be worked in the same manner and with as little effort. Make it a practice, however, to spread the stitches on the right needle to their full width before working the alternate color. This move allows the waiting yarn to strand completely behind the just-worked stitches, and your two color knitting won't pucker.

Weaving—Knit Stitches.

If you select a design with a series of 5 or more stitches in one color, you may weave the waiting yarn rather than strand it on the inside. The longer the strand, the harder it is to control tension.

To weave the color not in use is to carry it along as you work; it is never more than one stitch back, thus there are no strands. Weaving, as you know, is an under, over, under, over, movement. The good news is that you are already doing the unders, unconsciously, as you work a normal right or left hand stitch. That means you have to be conscious only for the overs. In a series of 5 stitches of one color, for example, work stitches 1, 3, and 5 normally, and use the weaving technique on stitches 2 and 4.

METHOD: Work only on *every other stitch* in a series.

To weave the left yarn while knitting with the right:
- Put the *right needle in*.
- Put the *left yarn gently over* the tip of the right needle.
- Put the *right yarn around* to make a stitch.
- Bring the *right stitch through*.

Put the right needle in and put the left yarn gently over the tip of the right needle.

Put the right yarn around to make a stitch, and bring the right stitch through.

To weave the right yarn while knitting with the left:
- Put the *right needle in.*
- Put the *right yarn around* as if to make a stitch.
- Put the *left yarn over* the tip of the right needle—from under.
- Take the *right yarn back to the back*—the way it came.
- Bring the *left stitch through.*

Put the right needle in, put the right yarn around as if to make a stitch, put the left yarn over the tip of the right needle—from under.

Take the right yarn back to the back, bring the left stitch through.

Two essential steps must be taken before two color knitting is started.
- Put a marker on the needle to identify the absolute beginning of the rounds. This marker should be at the right seamline.
- Count, and recount, to be certain you have the correct multiple of stitches on the needle. This design is worked over a multiple of 8 stitches; be sure you have 64.

The two-color design coming up in the sampler has a series of 5 stitches in one color in rounds 1 and 5. In order to practice both of the procedures, switch yarns from hand to hand for round 5; the day may come when you must work 5 dark stitches followed by 5 light stitches.

To work the design, the colors have been translated to dark and light. Rename your yarns. One must be darker than the other. To start, put the dark yarn in the right hand. For round 5, switch the dark yarn to the left hand.

Bordar 18*

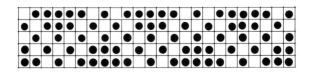

*Hans M. Debes, Foroysk Bingingarmynstur, p. 57.

METHOD: *(Round)* A multiple of 8 stitches. D = dark. L = light.
    Round 1—3D, *1L, 1D, 1L, 5D*, repeat * to *, ending 2D
           (instead of 5D).
    Round 2—2D, *1L, 1D, 1L, 1D, 1L, 3D*, repeat * to *, ending
           1D (instead of 3D).
    Round 3—*1D, 1L*, repeat * to *.
    Round 4—*1L, 1D, 1L, 3D, 1L, 1D*, repeat * to *.
    Round 5—*1D, 1L, 5D, 1L*, repeat * to *.

> *Work the 5 rounds of border design in the sampler.*
> *Work 2 rounds of stockinette stitch in original color.*
> *Repeat the round of alternating stitches to balance the border design.*
> *Work 6 rounds of stockinette stitch in original color.*

If using "the other hand" does not come naturally, be selective in your choice of color design. Scrutinize the patterns and settle for one in which one color predominates. Put the predominant color in the hand with which you usually knit, and put the color that works the fewer stitches in the other hand.

Directions for two color knitting are often written with the colors denoted as "main color" and "contrasting color." Rather than mentally struggling with that confusion, rewrite the pattern using dark and light; or, as you know the colors you are using, spell them right out—2 red, 1 white, etc. This aforethought step clears the air.

Designs may also be set up on graph paper, one square being equal to one stitch. This arrangement eliminates the need for words altogether, and the pattern may be used over and over in different color combinations. Many ready-made designs exist in this form; even a cross stitch design can be called into service. For further mileage and a totally different effect from one pattern, reverse the colors—work the dark as light, and the light as dark.

In round knitting, work a graph from the bottom up, reading the squares from right to left—unless otherwise directed. For flat knitting, work the graph from the bottom up, alternating the rows from right to left, and the next, left to right.

Two color designs written specifically for flat knitting may include an extra stitch for the end of the row that is excess baggage in round knitting. For the most part, a design that states it is a multiple of 8, plus 1, for example, can be trimmed to the exact multiple of 8. Please note the words *may* and *for the most part*; this is not an absolute occurrence.

Before leaving two color knitting, check the hand of this area of your sampler. If the fabric feels stiffer than in other sections, not thicker—which it is—but stiffer, work looser next time. Tension is of prime concern with two colors; too tight is more often the case than too loose. There is truth in that old adage about practice.

Weaving—purl stitches *(for future reference)* If your heart's desire is to knit a two color cardigan, and further, if your pattern has a series of 5 or more stitches in one color, you may need to weave the waiting color on a purl row.

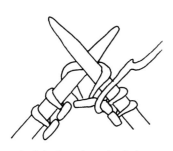

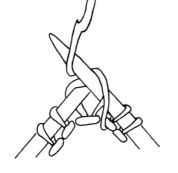

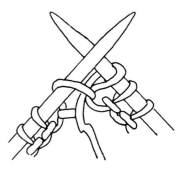

A right hand purl stitch.

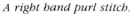

A left hand purl stitch.

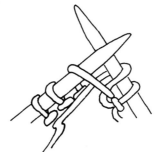

METHOD: Work only on *every other stitch* in a series.
To weave the left yarn while purling with the right:
• Put the *right needle in.*
• Put the *left yarn gently over* the tip of the needle.
• Put the *right yarn around* to make a stitch.
• Bring the *right stitch through.*

Final step in weaving the left yarn while purling the right: bring the right stitch through.

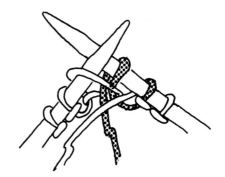

To weave the right yarn while purling with the left:
- Put the *right needle in.*
- Put the *right yarn around* the needle from below.
- Put the *left yarn over* as if to make a stitch.
- Take the *right yarn back to the front*—the way it came.
- Bring the *left stitch through.*

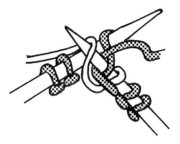

Having put the right yarn around the needle from below, put the left yarn over as if to make a stitch.

Two color knitting in the flat also rears its ugly head in the yoke of an otherwise round sweater, for once the neck shaping starts you are working back and forth on the needle. The Crew Neck requires the fewest back and forth rows, the low V Neck the most. Plan ahead to detour this inevitable shift by interspersing plain stripes with two-color patterns throughout the round knitting and then, from the neck shaping work only the plain stripes. The uninitiated won't realize why, nor perhaps even notice, that the two-color knitting stopped. Let them think you planned the sweater this way—which you did. True, you forfeit an all-over two-color design, but the sweater will balance and the two color patterns will speak even louder and clearer. Often, an all-over two-color sweater is just too all-over.

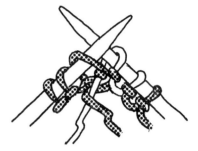

After taking the right yarn back to the front, bring the left stitch through.

Swiss Darning

Swiss Darning, also known as duplicate stitch, is an easy way to add more color to a completed sweater, embroider a monogram, create a plaid, or simply put a third color into a design worked with two. For the latter, select a logical stitch to cover, one that can be quickly spotted as you work. To avoid long strands spoiling the neatness of the inside, wiggle the yarn from one stitch to the next under the purl bumps.

The disguising powers of Swiss Darning will correct a color error, or a stubborn nonconforming stitch at a seam line. And for handspinners, it will camouflage a too-thin stitch.

METHOD: Thread a Braidkin or a blunt needle with a yarn of the same diameter in another color.

- From the inside, pull the yarn to the outside up through the center of the stitch *below* the one to be covered.

- Slide the Braidkin under both sides of the stitch *above* the one to be covered.

Swiss darning.

- Take the yarn back to the inside through the center of the stitch *below* the one to be covered—where it came up.

- Adjust the tension of this cover stitch.

> **Work a third color into the Scandinavian Design.** Cover the center stitch of the triangle formed by the dark yarn with a third color.

Now, take a brief break from the sampler.

The Knitted Cord*

The knitted cord.

The uses of this three stitch knitted cord are endless—depending on how much of it you can stand to do: tie bows, thread cables, lace cardigans, connect mittens, form monograms, tie hats, or work drawstrings, to name a few.

METHOD: Use 2 double-pointed needles—garment size.
- Cast on 3 stitches. (For this special technique, do not slip the first stitch.)

- *K3, Freeze. Do not turn your work. Slide* the 3 stitches to the other end of the needle. Give the yarn a gentle tug.*

- Repeat * to * for the desired length.

- To bind off: K1, K2 tog., pass the first stitch over the second, secure the yarn, and tuck in the tail.

> **Work about 2 feet of cord in the dark yarn,** and then it's back to the sampler. You need a place to put it.

The twisted cord *(for future reference).* A quicker cord, but not as substantial, is the twisted cord.

METHOD: Measure a strand of yarn 4 times the desired length of the finished cord.

- Double the strand.

- Tie one end around a doorknob, shut it in a drawer, or find someone to hold it.

- Walk as far away as the doubled strand allows.

*Elizabeth Zimmermann, *Knitter's Almanac,* p. 105.

- Twist, twist, and twist some more, until the twist runs tightly to the end in your hand.

- If the double strand is short enough (or, your arms long enough), hold it taut, grab it in the middle, and walk to the secured end. Hold the secured end with the loose end and release your grip on the middle allowing the doubled strands to twist together.

- If the doubled strand is too long (or your arms too short), find someone else to grab the middle.

- Tie an overhand knot one inch from each end. Cut the folded end and trim the ends an equal distance from the knot.

The Lacing Round Or Row

At wrists, necks, waists, or wherever you want or need a lacing, work the YO, K2tog. Here, as for the buttonhole, the YO leaves an opening large enough for a knitted cord of the same yarn; complementary proportioning. Or, if you and the sweater prefer, the lacing may be a twisted cord, a velvet ribbon, or a length of rawhide; whether it is truly functional or merely decorative is up to you. Due to their very stretchy nature, cotton sweaters thrive with a lacing above the body ribbing—a better accent and a quicker solution than threading their innards with elastic.

METHOD: The lacing round, or row, is worked on the outside.
Round. On an even number of stitches, YO, K2tog., around. On the next round, knit all the stitches.

Flat. On an uneven number of stitches, work:
   Row 1—Slip 1, *YO, K2tog.* Repeat * to * across the row.
   Row 2—Slip 1, purl all the stitches across the row.

> *Work a lacing round in the sampler.*
> *Work 5 rounds of stockinette stitch.* You have reached the top!

The technique for a picot edge on a hem is the same as a lacing. Take a minute to fold the last few plain rounds to the inside, check the appearance of the edge and file it in your visual memory. Then stand the top right back up again.

> **Insert the knitted cord into the lacing round.**
> Don't pull it tight yet.

Coming up next is The Knitted Belt, a close relation of The Knitted Cord. Put the sampler aside again for a minute.

The Knitted Belt *

The Knitted Belt is so much more than just a belt; think of it also for straps, suspenders, loops (belt, that is), and trims. As in The Knitted Cord, the yarn comes from the third stitch back at the beginning of every row to give a nicely rounded edge to both sides of this sturdy, reversible belt. You must work 2'' or 3'' of it before it begins to shape up—keep tugging down.

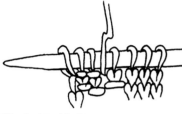

The knitted belt.

METHOD: Use 2 double-pointed needles—garment size.
- Cast on 7 stitches. (For this special technique, do not slip the first stitch.)

- *K4, bring the yarn to the front, slip the next 3 stitches as if to purl. *Turn* your work, and give the yarn a gentle tug.*

- Repeat * to * for the desired length.

- On the last row, knit all the stitches.

- *To bind off:* Slip 1, P2tog., pass the slip stitch over the purl; P1, pass the purl stitch over the purl; P2tog., pass the purl stitch over the purl, P1, pass the purl stitch over the purl. Secure the yarn, and tuck in the tail.

> **Work The Knitted Belt long enough to button through that gigantic belt loop, alias Sweatshirt Pocket.**
> **Add a buttonhole* in the last inch.**
> *Buttonhole Row—K3, YO, K2tog., bring the yarn to the front, slip 2 as if to purl.

The Sweatshirt Pocket itself would be an inadequate belt loop. But, a proper belt loop may be worked using the pocket technique—if you are able to judge the correct position of the loop, or loops, as you work a sweater.

*Elizabeth Zimmermann, *Wool Gathering, #21*, September, 1979.

The belt loop *(for future reference).*

METHOD: Stop working within 7 stitches of the top of the loop.
- Trace the next stitch down to where you want the loop's bottom.

- Slide a double-pointed needle through one-half of the next 7 stitches, heading left.

- With new yarn, and garment size double-pointed needles, work the Knitted Belt over the 7 stitches until you reach the top.

- Put one needle in front of the other, and knit the stitches together; presto, a sturdy belt loop to match that sturdy belt.

 A fool-the-eye placket neck, or a mock cardigan for that matter, can be engineered in the same manner on a crew neck sweater. Briefly, as you must have the idea by now:

 Work the pick-up round for the neck ribbing to within the center 7 stitches of the front.

 Travel down as many inches as you want for placket length, or go all the way back to the row above the ribbing for a cardigan.

 Knit up the next 7 stitches, and work the Knitted Belt to the top. Join it to the waiting stitches and complete the neck ribbing.

 Don't bother to work buttonholes—simply sew buttons at appropriate intervals through the belt and the sweater itself; a move which also attaches the two.

 Now, back to the sampler and on to its endings.

 To work the last round of any circular needle project, use an independent double-pointed needle in place of the right end of the circular needle. Your ending, whether it be a simple cast-off or something more elaborate, will proceed much quicker and steadier as you will have more control over the tension; a circular needle tends to drag as it empties. For the sampler (or for a sweater), with the outside facing you, take the right end of the circular needle and tuck it down into your work. Find a double-pointed needle the same size, and use it in your right hand.

 The sampler has 4 endings each worked over 16 stitches. As the first three are worked in the dark yarn, take your working yarn and send it down into the sampler with the needle: don't break it off for you will need it again.

The Knitted Cord Cast-Off*

 In a sweater worked from the bottom up, the use of the Knitted Cord Cast-Off* is limited to trimming necklines. An alternative to ribbing, it magically surrounds the openings with a welt-like edge of yarn while casting off the stitches; a soft and gentle ending for a sweater. Once implanted in the knitting mind, the application of

---

*Elizabeth Zimmermann, *Knitter's Almanac,* p. 110.

the Knitted Cord will certainly expand to other projects that would benefit from its finishing touch.

Now that you have worked the Knitted Cord on its own, you will better understand how it works as a cast-off. Set-up is important, so check it before you start:

With the outside of the sampler facing you, and with the right end of the circular needle and the working yarn tucked down inside, take the dark yarn, and this time, for security, knot it through the first stitch on the left needle.

Insert the double-pointed needle in your right hand between the first two stitches on the left needle and proceed to:

METHOD: Cast 3 stitches onto the left needle (with the dark yarn).
- *K2 (dark), K2tog. (1 dark, 1 light). Slip the 3 (dark) stitches back onto the left needle, being careful not to twist them.*
- Repeat * to *.

To start casting-off, it may seem strange to be casting-on, but the cord is an extension of the fabric. The 3 dark stitches should be sitting ahead of the other stitches on the left needle. Each time you knit the last dark stitch together with a light stitch you are getting rid of, or casting-off, 1 stitch of the sampler, and at the same time, adding a round knitted edge. The technique, of course, can be worked in selfsame color; the dark yarn is used here for clarity.

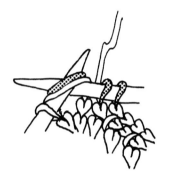

Cast 3 stitches onto the left needle.

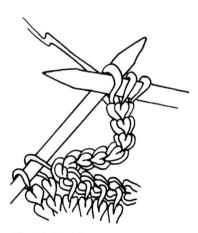

K2, K2tog.

> **Cast-off 16 stitches with Knitted Cord.**
> **Work a Knitted Loop at the 16th stitch.** See below.

The Knitted Loop

After casting-off the 16th stitch, do not return the 3 stitches to the left needle.
- Take another double-pointed needle, and work the Knitted Cord alone; that is, *K3, Slide *, and repeat for 2''.
- Put the empty double-pointed needle aside.
- Insert the left end of the circular needle into the 16th stitch again. You will be reworking this stitch to draw the base of the loop together.
- Slip the 3 stitches from the double-pointed needle onto the left needle, and K2, K2tog.
- Immediately cast-off the cord: slip 1, K2tog., pass the slip stitch over the knit stitch.
- Break the yarn, and snug the base of the loop together even more while tucking in the end.

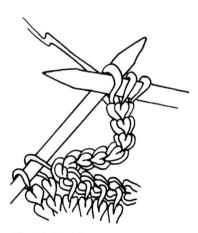

The Knitted Loop.

The loop alone deserves a home in your knitting bag of tricks; perhaps not as part of a neckline cast-off, but then again, why not?

The lucky sweater might spend less time lying on the floor. And, how about the cap that's lying there beside it, a useless pompon affixed to its peak. Think of all the time, and yarn, a loop would save; you could even make one while you're looking for the cardboard. On your next cap, worked and decreased in the round, reduce to a final 3 stitches, work a 2'' cord, cast it off, bend it over, and secure it to the inside with the tail. Then, side by side, cap and sweater will find their place hanging on a peg.

Hang everything; the mittens, the scarves, the wash cloths, the pot holders, and by all means, the Christmas stockings. If you don't have 3 convenient stitches at the ready, find them. Dig in around the edge of whatever, and with a double-pointed needle manufacture 3. The Shakers had the right idea—if it moves, hang it; assign it to a wall—their credo for a neat and tidy house.

Knitted cord edge—after the fact *(for future reference).* It is never too late to add a Knitted Cord Edge to a garment. This versatile trim may be worked on an existing cast-on edge, or a previously bound off edge, or, for that matter, up and down, or right around the middle of a finished sweater. Proceed stitch by stitch in whichever direction you decide to go. If perchance you do use the cast-off version for a neckline trim, the other sweater edges can be made to match. Plan ahead, and start the body and the sleeves without a ribbing pattern; but who knows, a knitted cord edge might settle onto a ribbed edge too. There are no specific directions for working this after-the-fact edging onto the sampler; however do try it someplace when you're through; either around the cast-on, or anywhere around the middle.

METHOD: Use 2 double-pointed needles—garment size.
- Cast on 3 stitches.
- Slide the left end of the left needle—the one with the stitches— under one-half of the stitch that marks the starting point for the trim. Slide the 4 stitches together, in a row, to the right end of the left needle.
- *K2, K2tog. Do not turn your work. Transfer the empty needle to your right hand. Again, slide the left end of the left needle under one-half of the next stitch to be worked.*
- Repeat * to *.

Knitted cord edge—after the fact.

Lace Cast-Off

Nothing changes the picture of a sweater more quickly than a dash of lace. Whether the yarn is a shimmering synthetic, a rough wool, a fluffy angora, or a dull cotton, the impact is instant: the sweater goes from plain to fancy. Yet, the beauty of this lace edge is in its working; for as it imparts its very special touch, inching its way around a neckline, it is also casting off the stitches. What more could you ask?

Lace edgings are usually worked, and consequently pictured, in very fine cotton thread. Keep this fact in mind when selecting a pattern to trim a sweater, for in a heavier yarn they will naturally be much deeper, and could be overwhelming. The pattern you are about to work is the very first, and the narrowest, in Barbara Abbey's book, *Knitting Lace.** Though worked with a base of only five stitches, it provides ample width for a lace edge on a sweater.

Lace cast-off is worked in the same manner as Knitted Cord Cast-off, except you are working back and forth over the lace stitches, turning your work.

The odd-numbered rows must be worked heading away from the fabric. The even numbered rows must be worked heading in toward the fabric. It is only on the even numbered rows that the last stitch of the lace pattern is worked together with a stitch from the fabric itself.

Therefore, it takes 2 rows of lace pattern to cast off 1 stitch. Every row starts with a slip 1. Work this slip 1 as if to purl, yarn in front, take the yarn to the back for the next stitch. The YO2 to a right hand knitter is: put the yarn forward as if to purl, and then take it around the needle back to this position again.

Make note of one trouble spot: The only purl stitches are in rows 2, 4, and 6. These purl stitches are worked into the second half of the YO2 from the row before. Don't drop these long diagonal stitches off the needle by mistake; no matter what they look like, purl into them.

Again, set-up is important, so check before you start: With the outside of the sampler facing you, and with the right end of the circular needle and the working yarn still tucked down inside, take the dark yarn, and again, for security, knot it through the first stitch on the left needle. Insert the double-pointed needle in your right hand between the first two stitches on the left needle and proceed to:

METHOD: (#1 Very Narrow Edging*—5 stitches).

• Cast 5 stitches onto the left needle (with the dark yarn).
• Knit the 5 stitches. Turn your work.

> **Row 1**—slip 1, K1, YO2, K2tog., K1. Turn your work.
> **Row 2**—slip 1, K2, P1, K1, *K2tog.* (1 dark, 1 light). Turn your work.
> **Row 3**—slip 1, K3, YO2, K2. Turn your work.
> **Row 4**—slip 1, K2, P1, K3, *K2tog.* (1 dark, 1 light). Turn your work.
> **Row 5**—slip 1, K1, YO2, K2tog., K4. Turn your work.
> **Row 6**—slip 1, K5, P1, K1, *K2tog.* (1 dark, 1 light). Turn your work.
> **Row 7**—slip 1, K8. Turn your work.
> **Row 8**—cast off 4, K3, *K2tog.* (1 dark, 1 light). Turn your work.

*Barbara Abbey, *Knitting Lace,* p. 43.

• Repeat rows 1 through 8.

> ### *Work Lace Cast-off over the next 16 stitches.*
> As you are only casting off 1 stitch every other row, you must work the 8 rows 4 times. At the end of Row 8, you are back down to the original 5 dark stitches. Turn your work, and start right in with Row 1 again. (The knit row you worked immediately after casting-on was a one time measure to get you started in the right direction—Row 1 must head out.) On the very last row, cast off all 9 stitches of lace. At the last cast-off stitch, pull a large loop out, pass the whole ball of yarn through, and secure—this will save attaching once more.

Lace-edging—after the fact *(for future reference).* The sleeve and body edges of a sweater (as well as shawls, scarves, baby clothes, blankets, and other fancy goods), are all candidates for a lovely, lacy edging. As you now know, worked directly as a cast-off, the lace practically applies itself, and the give of the fabric extends from one area to the other without any constriction in between. To duplicate this effect so that sleeve and body lace looks and acts as neck lace requires the elimination of the cast-on row or round. This move can be accomplished in two ways: a. Think of it ahead of time, or, b. Don't think of it ahead of time.

a. For those of you who are organized, and know exactly to what edges you plan to add lace, you may start the sleeves and/or body with the Invisible Cast-on. This cast-on allows you to work in reverse, and ceases to exist once you do, leaving nothing in its wake but an available round, or row, of stitches heading in the opposite direction.

However, even some of the most organized knitters would rather run and hide than work this cast-on; the very mention of its name sends them scurrying. If you are one of these, take heart; Barbara Walker* has come to your rescue. A picture is supposedly worth a thousand *words,* but in this case, a picture would not even come close to her written description of the process; she clarifies it in words that number just over 800. Put yourself in her hands, and relax, the cast-on is not invisible until you take it out, you can see it as you work it.

Barbara Walker's Invisible Cast-On

METHOD:
• Take a length of string, more than enough to hold comfortably all necessary stitches.

*Barbara Walker, *Knitting From the Top,* pp. 72-74.

• With one needle and the end of your yarn, cast on one stitch, and place it near the needle point. Hold this needle in your right hand.

• With the same hand, hold the end of the string under, and against, the needle, so that the string passes in *front* of the ball end of the yarn. Keep hold of the string and needle together, throughout.

• Put the left hand around the long strands of both yarn and string, and keep hold of both, henceforth. Put the left thumb between yarn and string, *below* the point where the string crosses in front of the yarn. Bring the thumb forward, carrying the yarn on it.

• Put the left forefinger between yarn and string, and open it backward, carrying the string on it. You now have a diamond-shaped opening between yarn and string, with the yarn on the thumb toward you, and the string on the forefinger away from you. The other three fingers of the left hand continue to hold both strands against the palm.

• Dip the needle point down into the diamond-shaped opening and bring it up toward you, thus picking up a loop of yarn from behind onto the needle. This is the second stitch.

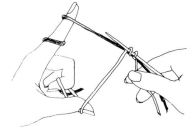

Second stitch.

• Without changing the position of the left hand, turn it over so that the back of the hand comes toward you. This reverses the positions of yarn and string: now the yarn, on the thumb, is at the back of the diamond, and the string, on the forefinger, is at the front. As you turn the left hand over, the yarn wraps itself *under* the string beneath the needle.

• Dip the needle point down behind the yarn, on the far side of the diamond, and bring it up *through* the diamond to put another yarn loop on the needle. This is the third stitch.

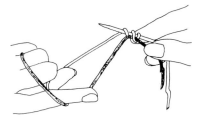

Third stitch.

• Still keeping the left hand in its position, turn it over away from you again, so that the yarn and string return to their original positions—yarn in front, string behind. As you do this, the yarn is brought forward under the string, which is still beneath the needle.

• Repeat Steps 6, 7, 8, and 9 for every subsequent pair of stitches, ending the cast-on with Step 8. There will be an uneven number of stitches, because the very first stitch on the needle is an extra one. If an even number of stitches is wanted, you can work "K2tog." at the end of *each* first row.

Now you have a lot of yarn loops over the needle and the string running along beneath the needle with the yarn twisted around it. Be sure the string has not been passed over the needle at any point and the loops on the needle are yarn only.

To work the first row, put the needle into the left hand, carefully holding the last cast-on loop on the needle meanwhile. Take the yarn *under* the string to the back, and begin the row, knitting all stitches through the front loops in the ordinary way. After 2 or 3 rows, you can see that the string is still holding exactly the same number of loops as the number of stitches cast on. Each of these loops will be a stitch to knit in the opposite direction. Leave the string in place until you are ready to pick up these loops onto a needle.

When you are ready to knit in the opposite direction, hold the work with right side facing, cast-on edge up. From the left, carefully slide the needle through all the loops that are on the string. Then pull out the string. Join the yarn at the right-hand edge and work the first row as follows: k1, * k1-b, k1; rep from *. The reason for knitting every even-numbered stitch through the back is that each of these stitches is twisted and must be knitted in back to straighten it out again. If you were to knit each of the even-numbered stitches in the front loop, it would be crossed at the base, like a normal "k1-b." This might provide a very acute observer with a clue concerning the place where you cast on. But without such a clue, no one in the whole wide world—not even the most expert of experts—can ever see the slightest trace of this cast-on row. Thank you, Barbara.

b. For those of you who do not like to commit yourself to going back and doing something on another end (and you really must—the invisible cast-on cannot remain as is), or, if lace is a sudden inspiration at the completion of a sweater worked with ribbings around its body or sleeves, you may snip one-half stitch in the round, or row, above that existing ribbing and **simply drop the ribbing off.** This procedure will also produce a round, or row, of stitches to which you may add a lace edge. The logic of this process, and the madness of the snipping method, is coming up in Afterthought Pocket.

By whichever means, a. or b., you have accumulated a needle full of stitches. Proceed exactly as for Lace Cast-off, i.e. cast onto the left needle the required number of stitches to work your selected pattern. Work 1 row of knit over the cast on stitches first, and then turn your work, so that Row 1 is heading away from the finished project. As a last resort, you could of course, work a lace edge directly onto the cast-on, or, as a matter of fact, onto a previous cast-off. Slide a needle into conforming strands of the finished selvedge to acquire a round, or row, of stitches, and there you are, all set to go. The drawback to this method is that you will have a restricting cast-on or cast-off between the fabric and the lace, and thus lose the fluidity of one to the other. Losing this oneness also diminishes intrigue, for it will be quite obvious that the lace was worked as an addition. Conversely, a scarf, or stole, for instance, with lace worked as a cast-off at each end, will look as if it had no beginning.

To reflect on a lace edge for sweaters brings to mind an elegant petticoat, so trimmed, that is hidden away in the archives at Sturbridge Village.* A garment that would be as stylish today as it was when made of handspun, handwoven fabric dyed scarlet, enhanced with a wide lace hem knit of the same yarn. Weavers take note: the next time you purchase yarn for a fabric, buy extra; weave a longish skirt and work a border of handknitted lace. In this instance, the lace could be worked separately and sewn on, unless you are inclined toward a crochet hook and could thereby work a round of loops on the edge of the fabric from which to start.

The cable stitch cast-off *(for future reference).* If a lace edge is, well, just too lacy, a border of cable stitch may be more to your liking. From other archives, namely the Franklin D. Roosevelt Library in Hyde Park, New York, comes the Cable Stitch Border.* Eleanor is remembered as "knitting, always knitting"—our own Madame LaFarge? Upon her death, her memorabilia joined Franklin's, and it will do your knitting heart good to see that the exhibit organizers recognized her "hobby" for what it was—and is to so many others—part of and inseparable from her daily doings. For there, an entire wall case displays her knitting paraphernalia. Behind the scene, in her personal papers, are hand written directions for the cable stitch border. Sent to her from an unknown admirer, the border was described as being "a marvelous way to attach bands for armholes, round, high necks, or wherever a contrasting band with a professional finish is desired." The writer further admonished that "A double border is lovely for a skirt hem when one is tall."

METHOD: The number of stitches to be cast off must be a multiple of 8. The border may be worked directly as a cast-off, or on stitches picked up around a previously cast-off, or cast-on edge. With the outside of the fabric facing you, and with a double-pointed needle in your right hand, insert the tip of the double-pointed needle between the first two stitches on the left needle (the one with the garment) and proceed to:

- Cast 12 stitches onto the left needle ahead of the stitches to be cast-off. Proceed immediately to:

> **Row 1**—Slip 1, P2, K6, P2, K2tog. (1 of border, 1 of fabric). Turn.
> **Row 2**—Slip 1, K2, P6, K3. Turn.
> **Row 3**—same as 1.

*Sturbridge Village, Sturbridge, Massachusetts 01566. An authentically restored rural New England village of 1790–1840.
*Eleanor Roosevelt Papers, Topical Files 1945–1962, Container 4642.

Row 4—same as 2.
Row 5—same as 1.
Row 6—same as 2.
Row 7—Slip 1, P2, Cable 6*, P2, K2tog. (1 or border, 1 of fabric). Turn.
Row 8—same as 2.

*Cable 6—Slip the next 3 stitches onto another double-pointed needle, or a cable needle; knit the next 3 stitches on the left needle. Return the 3 stitches on the extra needle to the left needle, and knit them.

Casting Off in Ribbing

The only casting-off in a sweater from the bottom up is the last round, or row, of ribbing at the neck edge. Casting off in your ribbing pattern, knitting the knits, and purling the purls, produces a zig-zag selvedge with a good amount of elasticity. If you tend to work this job tightly, use a larger size double-pointed needle in your right hand; looseness is vital especially to a crew neck sweater. In the sampler, the ribbing pattern will be K2, P2 worked back and forth over 16 stitches.

Start each row with a slip 1. This slip 1 will take the place of the first K1. Work it slip 1 as if to purl, yarn in back.

Check to be sure you are set up correctly: With the outside facing you, the dark yarn should still be attached at the end of the lace work. Using a double-pointed needle in your right hand, knit the next 16 stitches from the circular needle. (To have started in with K2, P2 in the dark color would have meant droopy purls). The ribbing will be less cumbersome to work if you use 2 double-pointed needles. Let the circular needle rest.

Turn your work after the knit row, and:

> **Work K2, P2, over the 16 stitches for an inch.**

To cast off:

METHOD:
- Slip 1, K1, pass the slip over the knit.
- Purl 1, pass the knit over the purl.
- Purl 1, pass the purl over the purl.
- Knit 1, pass the purl over the knit.
- Knit 1, pass the knit over the knit.
- Purl 1, etc.

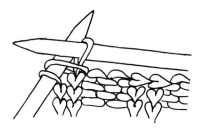

K2, P2 cast-off

> **Cast off the 16 stitches in K2, P2 ribbing.**

Now that the ribbing section is complete, note the difference in width between the 16 stitches cast-off in lace, and the 16 stitches cast off in ribbing. The lace produces almost twice the width of the ribbing.

To be prepared for the last ending, reach down into the sampler and pull out the original yarn. With a double-pointed needle in your right hand, and the inside of the sampler facing you, purl the remaining stitches. The circular needle is now empty. Put it aside, and work the remaining ending with 2 double-pointed needles.

Note—The purl row you have just worked is not the purl row for the turning edge of the hem coming up. It was worked to get you to the outside, and on 2 needles.

A Hem—Amen! You're almost through!

No decent sampler worth its salt should be left unsigned. Therefore, the last 16 stitches will be finished as a hem into which you may knit your initials. Not only is this a perfect ending for your sampler, but a hem is also a possibility for the ending of a crew or boat neck sweater; another alternative to ribbing. The hem may be worked plain, initialed, in a contrasting color, or with a picot edge. It affords you one last opportunity to personalize your sweater.

The initials charted here are 5 stitches high and 3 stitches wide; the smallest possible to knit. Most of the letters are legible; a few, such as N, leave a bit to be desired. Alphabets exist in many other larger, more ornate forms. Search the books, and start a collection. And, don't confine initials to a hem; think of sleeves and pockets too. To knit a monogram on a sweater front could be a bit of tricky business; for accurate positioning, Swiss Darning might be best.

> *Read through the directions for The Plain Hem and The Initialed Hem, and then proceed to the specific directions for working an initialed hem in the sampler.*

The Plain Hem

METHOD: (round or flat)
- Work 1 round, or row, of purl stitches on the outside for a turning edge. (In a contrasting color, remember to knit a round, or row first. For a picot edge, work a round, or row of YO, K2tog. instead.)
- Work 2 rounds, or rows, in stockinette stitch, decreasing the number of stitches by 10%. These evenly-spaced decreases ensure that the hem will lie flat when folded inside.

Decision point: the initialed hem. If your hem is to be initialed, see below before proceeding.

- Continue working in stockinette stitch for the desired hem depth. Do not cast-off the stitches.
- Break the yarn leaving enough to stitch the hem to the inside.
- Thread a Braidkin or a blunt needle, and lightly catch each stitch, one by one, to a purl bump on the inside.
- Work the stitching loosely so as not to constrict the give of the fabric. This stitching may be done with the stitches on the needle easing them off one at a time, or, if you're brave, pull the needle first. That's it.

The Initialed Hem

Graph the desired initials following the chart using 5 squares for height and 3 squares for width. Space each letter 1 stitch apart from its neighbor. The total width for 3 initials thus equals 11 stitches. Select a likely spot for them to occupy in the hem.

METHOD: Work the initials with a contrasting color.
Round. Read the graph upside down, from the bottom to the top. Work each round from right to left.

Flat. Start working the initials on an outside row. Read the graph upside down, from the bottom to the top. Work rows 1, 3, and 5 from right to left (the knit rows), and work rows 2 and 4 from left to right (the purl rows).

With the 5 rounds or rows of initial work complete, return to the directions for The Plain Hem.

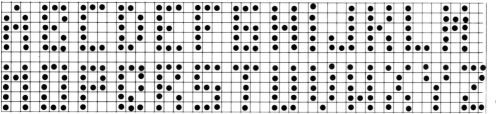

Graph—initials.

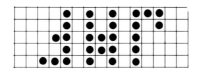

Example—initials for sampler hem.

> ***Now, for that hem in the sampler:*** (It's flat knitting, so slip the first stitch of every row.) With the outside facing you, and with the sampler yarn, work a purl row over the remaining 16 stitches for a turning edge.
> - Purl one more row.
> - Knit 1 row decreasing 1 stitch by starting, slip 1, K2 tog.*
> - Purl 1 row.
> - Set up your initials on graph paper, or a scrap, as per The Initialed Hem.
>
> The 3 initials, or 11 stitches, are worked in the center of the 15 stitches of your hem. Follow the flat directions for reading the graph. This is a taste of back and forth knitting with 2 colors; not as carefree as in the round. Bring the new color from under the old when changing from one to the other, to avoid holes.
>
> Work at least 2 rows beyond the initials before tacking down the hem.

*Attention flat knitters—which is all of you at the present moment. As Elizabeth would say, it is a GOOD THING that you had to decrease this one stitch. No mention has yet been made about decreasing at the beginning and/or end of a row. ***Don't.*** "If the book says" decrease 1 stitch at the beginning and/or ending of a row, ***never, ever,*** decrease right on the selvedge; move the decrease in a stitch or two. In other words, start the row slip 1, ***K2tog.*** work across to within 3 stitches of the end, ***SSK,*** K1. Your decreases have been worked, and your selvedge remains intact.

If your selvedge is wider, say with Cardigan Border, or any such else edging, work the decrease immediately after and immediately before the border. For example, with Cardigan Border start the row with the 6 stitch border, ***K2tog.,*** work to within 8 stitches of the end, ***SSK,*** work the 6 stitch border. Moving the decreases in from the edge will still narrow the fabric, and in a much more orderly fashion.

Afterthought Pocket*

Put pockets everywhere; in new sweaters, or in old favorites; in hand knits, or machine mades; in plain sweaters, or sweaters in a pattern—just be sure to snip the up-coming stitch to be snipped in a fairly calm row. Men love them, especially if built to a specific size for whatever their need, or, in any case make them deep enough

*Elizabeth Zimmermann, *Knitting Without Tears,* p. 37.

to be useful. Children love them in unexpected places; in a mitten, on a hat, or in a sleeve, a pocket becomes a secret hiding place for a special treasure. And, if you truly have a treasure to hide, or, simply a little mad money to keep out of sight, don't just graft that sweater underarm; work a pocket—a pit pocket. Who would ever think to look there?

In a sweater, the pocket may be worked anywhere. Try the completed sweater on to determine exactly where you want the pocket opening. Mark the stitch that is the center of the opening with a safety pin.

In the sampler, the pocket will be worked in the open area of the back beside the placket.

To position the pocket in the sampler: With the back of the sampler facing you, and the placket on your right, count 10 stitches to the left of the last purl stitch of The Cardigan Border. Put a safety pin through the stitch.

> **Follow the directions for The Afterthought Pocket line by line.**

METHOD: Snip one-half of the stitch that marks the *center* of the pocket opening.

- With the tip of a double-pointed needle, carefully lift the cut end of the yarn out of 5 1/2 stitches to the right and 5 1/2 stitches to the left of the center opening. (The reason for the 1/2 stitch: As you unravel horizontally, you can see that the yarn goes through each stitch twice. It is not necessary to completely free the last stitches. In fact, it is best if you do not. Leaving the yarn half in the last stitch makes the final neatening of the opening easier).
- Do not cut the loosened yarn ends. With a crochet hook tuck them out of your working way at each end of the opening. The pocket is worked on 4 double-pointed garment-size needles.

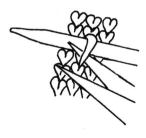

Snip one-half stitch.

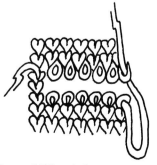

Unravel 5½ stitches to the left and right.

- Pick up the loosened stitches around the opening as follows:
- Slide a double-pointed needle through the 12 stitches at the bottom of the opening.
- Slide a double-pointed needle through 6 stitches at the top of the opening.
- Slide another double-pointed needle through the remaining 6 stitches at the top of the opening.
- Connect a ball of yarn at the first stitch on the right end of the bottom needle; knot it through if you wish.

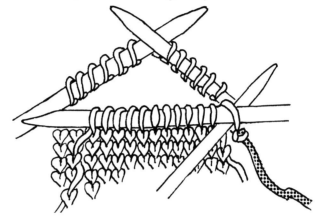

The pocket stitches on 3 double-pointed needles with the yarn connected.

- *Purl* across the bottom stitches only for a turning edge. (If you opt to work the pocket in another color, knit the bottom stitches this first time by, and purl them on the second pass). Proceed to the top stitches and from now on *knit* round and round all the stitches giving the yarn a good tug from needle to needle, especially at the corners of the opening.
- Work the pocket for 2'' in the sampler. In a sweater, work it to the desired depth.
- On the last round, combine the top stitches onto one needle.
- Break the yarn, leaving about 1 yard, and thread the end through a Braidkin, or a blunt needle.
- Turn your work, so that when facing you the yarn is coming from the first stitch on the right end of the needle farthest away from you. This needle is to become The Back Needle. Thus, the needle nearest you is The Front Needle.

You are now in a position to Graft the pocket bottom together—in a minute.

Grafting

Grafting, also known as Kitchener Stitch, is a method of constructing an invisible seam in your work; in this case, in stockinette stitch. This method has fewer steps than other written versions; it achieves the same effect with fewer motions. If grafting has discouraged or confused you before, give this way a try.

In a sweater, the technique comes into play to join the underarm stitches of the body to the sleeves. It is the ultimate touch that preserves the sweater's seamlessness, and therefore allows for it to be reversible. The specific set-up for grafting the sweater underarm stitches is detailed at that point in The Basic Sweater; what follows are a few generalities.

The edges to be joined must have an equal number of stitches. The stitches must be on the needle the way you would knit them; a twisted stitch will mar the perfection of the joining. The grafting is worked on the outside of the stockinette stitch fabric with the opening in a horizontal position. To start the grafting process the yarn must be coming from the first stitch at the right end of the back needle. Which is where you are.

> ### Follow the directions for Grafting line by line.

Note: Work the grafting loosely, for two reasons:

1. To attempt the proper tension as you work invariably leads to a row of tight stitches that restrict the give of the fabric. In a sweater at the underarm, the fabric must have give. Worked loosely, the "new stitches" may be adjusted to the tension of the fabric when the grafting is complete.

2. Grafting produces an invisible seam. To work it loosely is your insurance that you can backtrack, if necessary, to correct an error. Otherwise, you won't know what stitches to undo.

METHOD: *Important:* you are slipping the stitches as if to knit or purl, not actually knitting or purling them!

- *Slip the first stitch on the Front Needle onto the Braidkin as if to knit; let it sit there while you slip the Braidkin through the second stitch as if to purl; pull the yarn through. The first stitch is now *off* the knitting needle and gone. The second stitch is still *on* the knitting needle.
- Head for the Back Needle, keeping the yarn under the tip of the Front Needle.
- Slip the first stitch on the Back Needle onto the Braidkin as if to purl; let it sit there while you slip the Braidkin through the second stitch on the Back Needle as if to knit; pull the yarn through. The first stitch is now *off* the knitting needle and gone. The second stitch is still *on* the knitting needle.

  Note: Even though you are making two consecutive moves on each needle, you are doing away with only 1 stitch.

- Head for the Front Needle, keeping the yarn under the tips of the needles.*
- Repeat * to * until you have 1 stitch on each needle.
- Slip the stitch on the Front Needle onto the Braidkin as if to knit, slip the stitch on the Back Needle onto the Braidkin as if to purl, pull the yarn through both stitches.

Once you have worked the Grafting process a few times, the mental process will boil down to:

The Front Needle—Knit off, purl through.
The Back Needle—Purl off, knit through.

Or, you may find a better short thought.

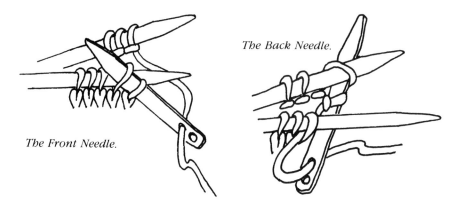

The Back Needle.

The Front Needle.

Worked loosely, the new stitches should be visible. To ensure proper tension, hold your left hand under them, as a darning egg. (Anyone remember how?) With the tip of the Braidkin, lift the stitches one by one to tension starting where you started and ending where you ended. Pull the excess yarn through and take it to the inside. Secure, and tuck in the end. Poke the pocket to the inside and neaten the corners of the opening with the unraveled ends. (In retrospect, you can see why the center stitch of the opening was snipped. Otherwise, you would have had a long end on one side and nothing on the other.) There are no rules for this operation, but the less done the better. Circle the yarn around each corner with a crochet hook, and gently ease any hole out of existence.

Done, with the exception of:

The Ends

To tidy the sampler, take the assorted yarn ends to the inside and with a crochet hook run them diagonally under a few purl bumps for about an inch. To level the jog in the cast-on round, take the tail of the slip knot through the lower stitch beside it before taking the end to the inside.

In the working of your sweater, always leave 5" or 6" ends, if possible. They'll be easier to find and handle for the final clean-up. Tuck them in as is with a crochet hook, sharp needle, or a Braidkin. Or, if the sweater is to be reversible, split the plies and head the ends diagonally in opposite directions. In either case, the ends should be snipped no shorter than 2" from their point of origin. Ends at crucial points should be even longer; you never know when a pocket corner, a sleeve cuff or a neckline might need a minor repair—an extra inch or two could save the day. And, lastly, don't

hide the ends from yourself; be consistent as to their burrows, and you'll know where to find them.

Your sampler is complete. ***Give it a good, strong, lengthwise tug.*** This tug will shape up its stitch combinations, most especially the ribbings; the purl stitches should hide. Now, take a minute to study your travels with 64 stitches; from wide to narrow, and wide to narrow again. Sometimes with your help—increases and decreases; and sometimes without your help—ribbings, and garter stitch, the latter two simply acting to their own inclinations. Now it's time to act to yours. With the sampler's options at your fingertips, it's on to the sweater. Your choice of yarn, the proper tools, and some straight thinking will guarantee its success.

EQUIP YOURSELF

Yarns

The world of yarn is now your oyster. With a free spirit and from a cast of thousands, you may select your sweater yarn. Well, almost a free spirit. Stemming from the premise that the yarn be worthy of your time, there are two factors that deserve your consideration; content and ply.

Starting with content, a natural fiber is best. Underground concoctions will never reproduce that which grows or walks above; wool, cotton, linen, silk, angora, mohair, alpaca, cashmere, camel hair, and yes, even dog hair, are the most promising candidates. Wool topped that list on purpose: there is no substitute for its warmth, protection, longevity, color range, and variety of texture. The assortment is tremendous; every country seems to have a specialty—a yarn distinctive to its region. Of all the natural fibers, wool is the most versatile. It may be as thin as a cobweb for a light evening sweater, or as thick as a cord for one of massive proportion. Wool blends with other natural fibers, and also with synthetics; how successfully with the latter is difficult to say—word of mouth may be your best reference.

The popularity of a wool/synthetic, or a synthetic alone is, of course, its affinity to the washing machine. Perhaps it is possible to toss in acrylics full cycle, but what matter? They are what they are, never to be confused with, nor be a replacement for, a wool sweater. They don't wear like wool, act like wool, feel like wool, look like wool, last like wool, or knit like wool.

As opposed to wool, cotton produces a year round, any season sweater; cool in summer, warm in winter. (Lacking a down puff, try a cotton sheet or spread over a wool blanket some cold and blustery night—an insulation better than feathers.) Its dual properties are somewhat hampered by the limitation of its colors; available most often in light pastels and vivid brights, it associates with hot weather wardrobes. Noticeable too, is a difference in its very knitting. Lacking the spring of a wool yarn, cotton is likely to strain and tire your hands. Once knit however, the fabric has give; it stretches quickly when worn, and shrinks back to shape when washed.

Due to their scarcity, the remaining natural fibers approach the luxury level of knitting yarns, and understandably so. A cashmere sweater, for example, requires an amount of yarn equal to the annual fleece of two or three goats. On the contrary, the fleece of one sheep yields enough yarn for two or three sweaters. Expensive and elegant all, but treat yourself to their exclusiveness if only for a touch here or there.

Novelty yarns are in a class by themselves. Each outdoes the other with whirls and mixes of color, texture, and content; a sight to behold on the shelves. Irresistible, yes; but a word of advice to the less than flamboyant: proceed with caution. Purchase one skein and knit a sample—or even two or three. Then, pin them on and face the glass. What promised to be the last word compacted in a ball may speak too loudly expanded in a sweater. If so, confine its bid for power to the yoke, or a trim, remembering that a little bit of a good thing goes a long way. And, if its splendor ends up as decor in a basket, it is still a feast for the eyes.

The ultimate knitting thrill is to work with your own handspun yarn. An attachment develops between you and your offspring through the picking, carding, spinning, and plying—along with a respect for the tools and the process, not to mention the origin; the plant, the animal, or the worm. Anyone who holds a needle or deals with yarn should be required to go back to the source, follow the steps, and become familiar with the operation of wheels, handcards, niddy-noddys, swifts, clock reels, and the like. Avail yourself of the nearest spinning class, or head for a live demonstration. Perhaps the time-consuming task is not for you, fine. At least you will be knowledgeable about that with which you work, and better understand its properties.

Any natural fiber may be handspun alone, or carded with another. Again, wool is the leader for all the previous reasons, plus the availability of the fleece; the problem is not in finding one, but in resisting the urge for one more. The black sheep provides a range of values through the browns and grays as well as blacks. Whether to card the shades together or work them separately is the first Decision Point for spinners; in effect, the planning of a sweater takes place at that irreversible moment. Either way, the result is a truly unique yarn in the strictest sense of the word. No two fleeces are alike, no two spinners spin alike, and no two yarns are alike; originals, not to be duplicated.

The white sheep is indeed indispensible. Each breed has a characteristic staple, and its own interpretation of white—from white-white, through the pearly tones to cream. Used as is, or naturally dyed, it reflects its, or your, individuality. Who else has an off-white cardigan with a yoke of red clay pink, privet hedge green, and dandelion yellow?* Try to embroider a logo on that one, or give it a label; it parts company with the catalog crowd.

And, nonspinners, you don't have to sit back and admire these natural beauties from a distance. A commercial white, or off-white wool yarn will dye just as nicely. Go—pick flowers, gather nuts and pinecones, collect tree barks and onion skins; borrow or buy a good dye book; and set out on your own color adventure. Keep in mind one fact: any stuff that stains the hands, such as beets or berries, will not take fastly to the yarn. The best dyestuffs are the ones that give no hint as to what they will produce. Queen Ann's Lace, green and white, will magically bring forth a clear, sharp yellow. This is the fun, the suspense, and the mystery of natural dyeing—the unexpected outcome. Why not surprise your sweater with a stripe or two in hues commercial dyes cannot imitate?

Often overlooked as a source of unusual yarns for knitting are "so-called" weaving yarns. Don't be shy. Open the door to a shop with looms on display and you're certain to find yarns of substance and depth, interesting textures, and a better selection of natural fibers. Though they may look strange, wound as they are on a cone, most are perfectly adaptable for sweaters. Some that seem a bit rough or coarse will become soft and supple if washed first. Incidentally, herein lies the fundamental difference between a woven fabric and a knitted fabric. A woven cloth is not considered finished until it has been washed and fulled. Weavers accept this condition and therefore work directly from cone to loom allowing not only for the eventual shrinkage of the yarn itself, but for the pull-in of the fabric once released from the tension of the loom. Upon finishing, the fabric is cut and sewn to shape. Knitters do not figure a shrinkage allowance; the sweater/fabric must fit off the needles and remain the same size through washings. In short then, weavers wash last, knitters wash first, and should no matter the yarn; it's the only guarantee for success.

Coned yarn or any yarn can readily be skeined for washing with the aid of a niddy-noddy, the back of a chair, or even a bent arm. Tie the skein in several spots with figure-8's of cotton string to prevent tangling in the process. Wash the skeins in cool water with Woolite®, and in the same water temperature, rinse twice. Put to spin in the washing machine for one minute to remove the excess water, and hang to dry. (The procedure for washing a sweater is the same, except lay flat to dry.)

*Carol Conners, Janesville, Wisconsin.

The second factor to consider before making your yarn decision is ply. Plying is the twisting of single strands into one yarn; a 4-ply yarn is made up of four individual strands twisted together, a 2-ply is two strands, and so forth. Ply has nothing to do with the diameter of the yarn. A 2-ply yarn may be very fine or very thick, depending on the diameter of its individual strands. Yarn is plied to make it stronger; it goes without saying that a 2-ply yarn is stronger than either of its individual strands. It is also plied so that it will knit a straight fabric. For plying is usually done in the opposite direction from that in which the individual strands are spun. Reversing the twist helps to correct any overspin in the single strands. To knit with a single, overspun or not, can often result in a permanent bias slant to the fabric. Conversely, if the single strand is underspun, or too lightly spun, the yarn will pull apart as you knit, and the finished sweater will keep growing and stretching as it is worn. Contrary to popular opinion, a thick, lightly spun single does not produce a rugged sweater; it results in one of soft bulkiness. On a scale of 1-ply to 5-ply, it is the 5-ply tightly twisted yarn that is the most sturdy, attested to by the Scottish Ganseys that were worked from this yarn at nine stitches to the inch and survived from generation to generation.

For handspinners, plying also results in a more even yarn—if the thick and thin spots in the single strands conveniently meet their opposite in the process, and fortunately they usually do.

Having briefly touched on the quality of the yarn, the next question concerns quantity; how much of that favored yarn is needed for a sweater? The two factors to consider are the size of the sweater and the diameter of the yarn. The first is a simple matter, and the second will be shortly.

There ought to be a law that yarn be sold in fat and healthy 4 ounce skeins, or now that grams are in vogue, 100 grams. It is the varying amounts of yarn in a skein and the dual system of weights that causes confusing calculations. Who can cope with grams vs. ounces and deal with yarn in weird amounts? What good is one and five-eighths of whatever? Perhaps a revolt is in order against all those small balls, some even packaged in plastic. Handspinners have the definite advantage; they must and they do calculate on their own, and are free to think in ounces or grams at their pleasure. The amount of yarn needed can be determined in a fleeting second—the time it takes to plop a similar sweater on a scale. If it weighs in at 12 ounces, they must spin 12 ounces—easy as pie. As spinners do, so should you. Be brave; devise your own system of weights and measures. Invest in a scale. It needn't be a "legal" measure; it's for your own private use. An old baby scale—the wicker basket type—is perfect; or, a new one if you also have the proper occupant. Then, weigh your sweaters, and weigh the yarns, and make notes for future reference.

Or, if a scale is not in your immediate future, you can still estimate yarn amounts on your own; granted, with a little more thought. Most yarns can be categorized into three weights by diameter; fine, medium, or heavy. A sweater of a fine yarn requires fewer ounces than an equal size sweater in a medium yarn, for there are more yards to its ounce. Based on that fact, a rough calculation is possible. For instance, a size 40 sweater takes approximately 12 ounces of a fine yarn, 20 ounces of a medium yarn, and 28 ounces of a heavy yarn. As sizes go up and down by two's from 40, add or subtract 1 ounce for each size change in the proper category.

Heavy

Medium

Fine

The Diameter of the Yarn. *Yarn generally falls into one of three diameter categories: fine, medium, or heavy. Its diameter predicts the finished weight of the sweater. For purchasing purposes, categorize your intended yarn into one of the three, (as closely as possible), and refer to A Rough and Approximate Guide to Yarn Amounts.*

As stated, this measure is rough and approximate; but what harm? If you overcalculate you will have enough for a scarf or a cap; if you land under, your creative brain will have a chance to strut its stuff. At least, you won't be empty handed. For using a mental calculation allows you to buy yarn anywhere, any time, or any place. If you suddenly find yourself in the midst of a great sale, or make an unexpected stop at a mill, don't hesitate; buy all you can carry. Repeat, repeat, and repeat; 40 equals 12, 20, 28. Of course, it doesn't really, for they add up to 60—but you know what you mean. Etch it in your head, or on a scrap of paper, and may you never have to pass up a yarn bargain again. And, if the yarn obliges in 4 ounce skeins, you know in a wink that—for a size 40 sweater, you need three, five, or seven depending on its diameter. So, let's hear it for yarn in 4 ounce skeins—and that's the loose hank type, not the pull from the center variety. First, they make for fewer connections; second, they are ready for washing and/or dyeing; and third, they

A Rough and Approximate Guide to Yarn Amounts

Size	Fine	Medium	Heavy
46	15	23	31
44	14	22	30
42	13	21	29
40	12	20	28
38	11	19	27
36	10	18	26
34	9	17	25
32	8	16	24
30	7	15	23
28	6	14	22
26	5	13	21
24	4	12	20
22	3	11	19

simplify the math. To be perfectly honest, there is a fourth; they can be hugged.

Needless to say, there are some who object to yarn in loose skeins, for it must be balled before use. But, yarn doesn't come on a silver platter, or grow on shelves. It was alive, it is alive, and it will come alive in your hands. The least you can do is to take part in the very last step of its processing. It's your chance to avoid an otherwise sterile approach to its being. Open the skein, shake the strands loose, take a good look at it, squeeze it, feel it, talk to it (sweetly) as it runs through your fingers; become a part of it. It is nothing short of a miracle.

If you happen to be a non-stop knitter, and time is your biggest objection, a swift and a ball winder would pay for themselves in very short order. The swift holds the yarn and is adjustable to any size skein. It replaces the need for another pair of arms or the back of a chair. The yarn is wound around the tube-like projection on the ball winder thus allowing the yarn to collapse in the middle once the winding is completed. The end result is a soft ball of yarn that will sit in a stationary position beside you. Worked from the center, the yarn will continue to collapse and relax and be under

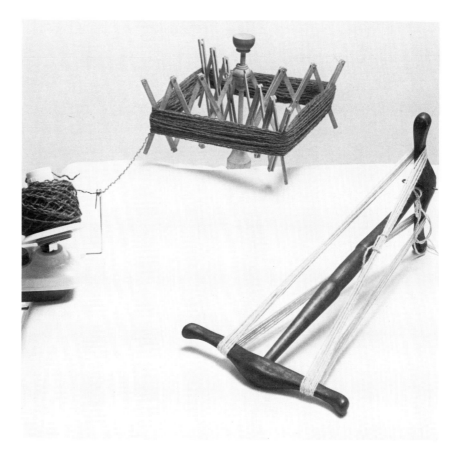

Skeining and Unskeining. *To skein yarn for washing and/or dyeing, a niddy noddy is the proper tool. Once the yarn is wound around, the ends are secured, and the skein is tied in four spots with figure 8's of cotton string to prevent tangling in the bath. The niddy noddy is also a measure, for once around is two yards.*

In combination, the swift and ball winder do the opposite job; that is they take the yarn from skein formation and transfer it into a pull-from-the-center ball that sits flat and upright.

a minimum amount of tension. Lacking these tools, wind the yarn by hand into a loose, yes, even sloppy looking ball. Avoid stress and tightness at all costs; keep it soft, soft, soft. Or, use the favored method of Japanese knitters* and wind the yarn into a loose cocoon. Under no pressure at all, the yarn is merely transferred from a non-workable skein into a workable skein-like arrangement. The cocoon lies flat and the yarn is worked back and forth from the *center*. As unbelievable as it sounds, it is possible to wind an entire 4 ounce skein around your left hand.

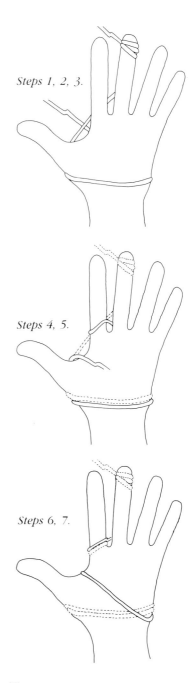

Steps 1, 2, 3.

Steps 4, 5.

Steps 6, 7.

The Yarn Cocoon:

Step 1: Borrow some arms, or place the skein around the back of a chair.

Step 2. Wind one end of the yarn around the tip of the middle finger of the left hand 3 or 4 times. With the palm of the left hand facing you, and the yarn behind the middle finger,

Step 3. take the yarn completely around the outside of the left hand via the base of the thumb, the little finger, and the forefinger.

Step 4. *Take the yarn to the back between the forefinger and the middle finger.

Step 5. Cross the back of the hand and bring the yarn to the front via the heel of the palm and around the outside of the thumb.

Step 6. Cross the palm heading for the heel.

Step 7. Cross the back of the hand and bring the yarn to the outside of the forefinger—repeat from * to *

Step 8. When the skein is completely wound around your left hand, tuck the working end under a few strands of yarn and secure.

Step 9. Remove the left hand.

Step 10. Start working with the end that was wrapped around the middle finger.

Needles

Circular needles, in combination with double-points, are all that are needed to knit a sweater, period. This fact will undoubtedly upset your knitting apple cart, especially if you have carefully, and finally, amassed a collection of knobby-ended needles. To be perfectly blunt, and it's about time someone was, long, straight needles are useless. The culprit who first put an end on a knitting needle was most likely an accomplice to whoever began writing sweater directions in pieces. Oh, for the pleasure of stringing them both up with some raveled yarn.

The yarn cocoon.

*Thank you, Sachiyo Nagasawa, Tokyo, Japan, a workshop student at the Rhode Island School of Design.

A dead-end, or one-way, needle not only interrupts the rhythm of your knitting, but also the rhythm of your sweater. For just as you are getting up to speed, you must come to a roaring halt, and your pattern is then in need of an interfering seam. Moreover, a knobbed needle hinders creativity. In contrast, a circular needle allows stitches to be slipped or knitted from one to the other, or, to be left "on hold" without a thought as to knitting direction. Other advantages are more obvious; a circular needle is lightweight, easy to use, and in one piece. It confines your work to the boundaries of your lap; no longer are you flapping those long, thin wings.

A well-rounded needle collection includes 16" and 24" circulars and sets of 8" double-points in sizes 3, 4, 5, 6, 7, and 8. Fill-in with the smallers and the largers if you are the type for very fine or very thick yarn; you are probably one or the other, not both. The shorter circulars work the sleeves and neck ribbings; the longers are used for the body proper, the body ribbings, and neck ribbings on occasion. When you have too few stitches for the 16" circular, the double-points substitute; worked in four's, they act as round. Individually, or in two's, they take over to perform the small jobs, and being two-way, they come to the rescue in strange situations. True, sweaters of seamless construction require five or six needle changes, but switching from one to the other becomes automatic by the second sweater, as long as you have them on hand. Nothing is more aggravating than not having the correct needle size when you need it. So, stock up. The cost is minimal compared to weaving a fabric; be glad you don't need a loom with all its trappings.

As for the needles themselves, those of metal are far superior to plastic. They are fast, smooth, and end up where they are aimed. Click they do, but only to announce progress; a quiet needle seems always at a standstill. Purchase needles singly, all of one brand or kind. Working a gauge sample on plastic and the sweater on metal, or vice versa, could affect your stitches-to-the-inch measure, for the plastic tend to be a tiny bit larger. Also, steer clear of prepackaged sets with screw-on ends. The end you want will always be busy on another project; who has the patience for that performance in the middle of a brainstorm? Be particularly fussy about the joinings; a circular needle is only as good as its connection. And, be aware that older, or much used, circular needles with color-worn ends may discolor your yarn. A light color yarn, especially white or off-white, may turn into a fabric streaked with black, and a natural dyed yarn may completely change color.

Miscellany

Braidkin. * The handiest little tool of all is the Braidkin. Long familiar to rug braiding enthusiasts for lacing braided strips together, the Braidkin belongs in the knitter's basket. Its blunt, angled tip slides under, around, and through stitches without splitting them, thus making a neat job of grafting, Swiss darning, and any other task requiring a needle. If at first you don't succeed and have to try again, it's a simple matter to flip the yarn back out as it is not hung up in the middle of a stitch. The Braidkin has two eyes, only one of which you must thread. If you're handy with a file, the two eyes could become one. Fine to medium weight yarns pose no threading problem.

Dental floss threader. ** This unusual piece of equipment comes to the rescue threading heavy weight or novelty yarns through the Braidkin. Put the yarn through the loop end, and then pull the straight end through an eye of the Braidkin. Keep these in a special place; they are invisible. Or, dab the end with nail polish, it helps to find them.

Tools of the Trade

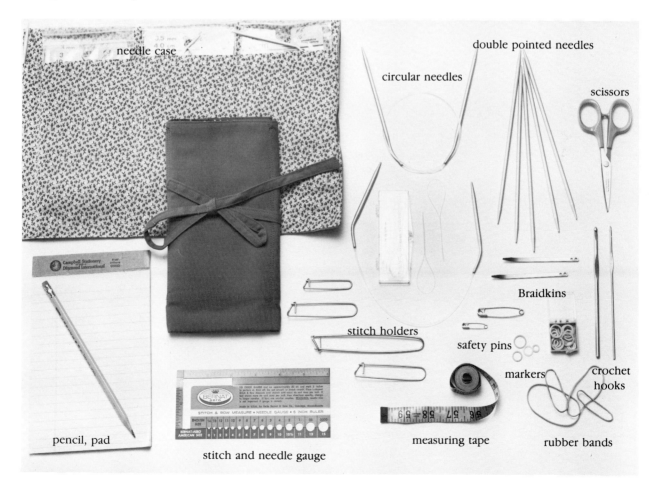

needle case · circular needles · double pointed needles · scissors · Braidkins · stitch holders · safety pins · markers · crochet hooks · pencil, pad · stitch and needle gauge · measuring tape · rubber bands

*Manufactured by Braid-Aid, Route 53, Pembroke, MA 02359
**Distributed by John O. Butler Co., Chicago, IL 60611

Needle gauge. This measure is an absolute necessity, and often has a built-in opening for counting stitches to inch. Once out of their cases, most circular and double-pointed needles are unidentifiable as to size and without a needle gauge they might very well remain homeless the rest of their lives. Be aware that German and English needles might fit a tiny bit loose in a U.S. gauge. German circulars, however, are marked in millimeters on the needle near the joinings—both ends. All you have to do is translate if mm's are not your forte.

Markers. Markers are another absolute necessity. Yes, they do keep hopping off the needle, but find another, and put it right back on again. Invest in the thinnest markers you can find; fat markers tend to distort the seamline. Yarn markers have their places, but in constant use they fray. And, in flat knitting they have to be flipped and flopped from one side of the work to the other. Limit their use to temporary positionings.

Scissors.   Crochet hooks.   Tape measure.

Stow this miscellany in a small zippered pouch and/or in the upcoming needle case.

Needle Conversion Chart

US	0	1	2	3	4	5	6	7	8	9	10	10.5	11
mm	2	2.5	2.75	3	3.5	3.75	4	4.5	5	5.5	6	7	8

The Needle Case [*]

This easy-to-make needle case is designed to hold all your circular and 8" double-pointed needles, as well as the above miscellany. When filled, it compactly folds into a case no bigger than a paper back book. Tuck it in a bag or a suitcase and you're off with all your knitting tools.

Materials:
  3/4 yard outer fabric
  3/4 yard inner fabric
Both fabrics should be firmly woven cottons—denim, calico, kettlecloth—wools, or corduroys in coordinating color/patterns.

Cut:
  (A) 1 19" × 18 1/2" piece of outer fabric for case.
  (B) 1 19" × 18 1/2" piece of inner fabric for case.
  (C) 2 19" × 8 1/2" pieces of inner fabric for pockets.
  (D) 2 1 1/2" × 15" pieces of outer fabric for ties.

Sewing Instructions:
Note—for sewers only: you may revert back to thinking right and wrong to describe the sides of the fabric.

[*] ©1979 Alice Beal. Thank you, Alice.

Pockets:

1. Hem one 19″ edge of each pocket piece. (C)
2. Place pocket pieces (C) right side up on right side of inner fabric piece (B).
3. Machine baste raw edges of pockets to inner fabric with a ⅜″ seam.

Ties:

4. Fold in ends and sides of tie pieces (D) ¼″. Press.
5. Fold each tie in half lengthwise, and press again.
6. Top stitch the ends and sides of ties.
7. Pin ties to the wrong side of the left edge of inner fabric 4½″ from top and bottom.

Case:

8. Lay outer piece (A) on top of inner piece (B) *right* sides together.
9. Stitch around all sides using a ½″ seam, leaving a 3″ opening on one 19″ side for turning.
10. Turn right side out, and press.
11. Top stitch around all edges.

Pockets:

12. Divide each pocket piece (C) into four equal sections by drawing chalk lines from the hemmed edge to the top and bottom of the case.
13. Sew a double row of stitches ¼″ apart through all layers to form pockets.
14. Press to finish. Fold in half, top to bottom, and then fold accordian style, and tie.

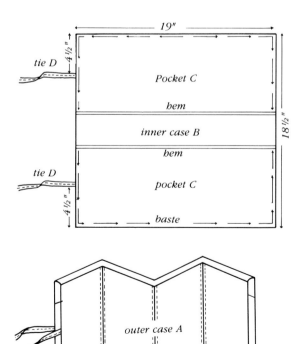

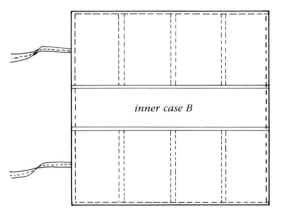

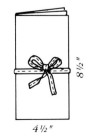

UNRAVEL YOUR THINKING

The Sweater Construction

Pure, logical, simple, sensible, easy, exciting and fun—all these words and more can be used to describe the construction of this sweater. Built to principles as ages old as any other form of shelter, the sweater is worked from the bottom up. It rises from a firm foundation, is worked round and round to the top, and is finished in the process; as an igloo of ice, a cabin of logs, or an adobe of brick.

For when it all began, this means of creating a fabric with sticks and fiber, survival was foremost. The motivating factor was need; immediate need for a protective body covering. And what could be simpler or quicker than a seamless garment instantly wearable directly off the needles? Apparently nothing, for the preserved remains of early undershirts and tunics in museums throughout Europe are proof that knitting had seamless beginnings. But, somewhere along the way that seamlessness began to come apart.

The practice of piecemeal construction dates from the birth of the cottage industries. For production purposes, each family member, or neighboring knitter, was responsible for one section of a garment, the whole being made from the parts. (Do you suppose they drew straws for the job at the end of the line?

The machinery of the Industrial Revolution perpetuated the piece-work construction of garments. Knitted fabric was loomed flat, as woven fabric, then cut to shape, and sewed together. Or, it was loomed full-fashioned—that is, loomed in pre-shaped pieces—and seamed together at the selvedges. Circular knitting frames produced tubular fabric of various diameters, but this fabric too, was cut and stitched for undergarments. Hosiery was the only exception.

In the late 1800's, directions for handknitted sweaters appeared on the scene and followed this flat knitting trend. Instructions were written to knit the front and back in one flat piece, up and over the shoulder, from either direction—increasing and decreasing for the neck. Side seams were sewn, and the sleeves inserted, or picked up at the armhole and worked down.

By the early 1900's, the front and the back had become disconnected altogether, and for the most part, have remained as separate entities to this day. Often, the result is dismaying. The vision of the perfect sweater vanishes with the reality of the finished garment, too long, too short, too loose, too tight, or, it is never finished at all; the pieces forever remain in a basket awaiting the sewing needle. For some, the enjoyment of knitting is gone.

This sweater brings back that lost pleasure. Its construction is such that it grows and develops the way you will wear it; try it on as you go. Work the body to the underarm, the sleeves to the underarm, then join the three tubes and head for the top. And, who's to know at the start how it will end? Options galore will pop into your head, a procrastinator's delight, until Decision Points are reached.

The firm foundation welcomes patterns; they originate from a given number of stitches and travel completely around with nothing to break their rhythm. The simplicity of the sweater's shape leaves it wide open for design; think color, contrast, line, or, take the easy way out and rely on nothing more than the texture of the yarn itself for interest.

Whatever, you will acquire a taste for thinking and knitting on your own, for the sweater will be you. And, it will fit. Gauge, coming up.

The Gauge Sample

The importance of gauge is stressed in every knitting book, magazine, pamphlet, and individual sweater pattern. You, the knitter, are warned and cautioned to work to the gauge of the sweater's designer. Some of you heed the advice, and some of you don't; but it's often a no-win situation in either case. Those who dutifully keep changing needles until the correct gauge is achieved may suffer through the sweater either cramping their knitting style, or being constantly on the alert to think loose. Those who barge ahead using the suggested numbers and needles may suffer the consequences of an ill-fitting sweater of a fabric that is either too stiff or too frail.

The variable lies in your hands. For as your fingerprint and signature prove, your hands are like no others; you each have your own knitting rhythm and tension. But, you often knit in isolation, filling quiet, solitary hours with the comfort of yarn and needles. This aloneness conceals the fact that the same yarn and needles in the hands of another results in a different gauge. If you were to knit in a room with twenty others, the fact would be obvious; twenty knitters could equal twenty sweater sizes. Find a friend. Knit together, and the need for a gauge sample will be self-evident.

Three Gauge Samples. *This trio of gauge samples clearly illustrates the need to work to your own gauge. The samples were worked with the* same *yarn, on the* same *size needles, over the* same *number of stitches, for the* same *number of rows. The obvious difference in their widths and lengths, and thus, to their stitches-to-the-inch, is attributable only to the three sets of hands working to their owner's individual knitting tensions—tight, loose, or somewhere in between. From left to right, Nancy Sladen, the author, and Anne Pompeo. Thank you, both.*

To knit on your own, you have no choice but to knit a gauge sample; for your gauge sample is the source of your numbers. It is also your assurance that you, your yarn, and the resulting fabric will be *content*. You may knit to your normal tension, your yarn will sit in its most comfortable position on whatever size needle best fits its contours, and the fabric may be as dense or as airy as you choose. In addition, the sweater this fabric becomes will be the intended size. And, this is the heart of the matter. For though, yes, you are knitting a sweater, you are in all actuality knitting a fabric in the shape of a sweater. You are a production line of one, for the finished fabric is a ready-to-wear garment requiring no further cutting or sewing. For this reason, the fabric must be appropriate to the sweater, and, *at the same time,* the completed sweater must fit the body.

The purpose of a gauge sample is to see to it that you achieve both goals in one operation; primarily it produces a sample piece of fabric, and secondarily, it serves as an accurate measure of stitches to the inch, the measure upon which the size of the sweater depends.

Here, in this one little knitting that takes about ten or fifteen minutes of your time, is the answer to the perfectly fitting sweater. It is not a boring procedure. To repeat, it is a preview of the delightful sweater to come. You may even become addicted to sampling. Sample everything.

The Definitions

All that remains between you and the sweater are a few definitions. Though they constitute a glossary, they are not in alphabetical order; they are in sensible order.

Read this page, as any page, and digest the terminology before you start; the meanings are paramount to the working of the sweater.

The fabric of your sweater, as any fabric, may be described as having a right side vs. a wrong side, a front side vs. a back side, or an outside vs. an inside. If these terms are used interchangeably in knitting directions, confusion arises. For right is not only the opposite of wrong, it is also the opposite of left. Front and back are not only the sides of a fabric, but are also used to identify the sections of a sweater. With that as food for thought, the following definitions are gospel to these directions.

Fabric. The material of a sweater.

Gauge sample. A sample piece of fabric.

Right. As opposed to left.

Left. As opposed to right.

Front. The front section of a sweater.

Back. The back section of a sweater.

Outside. The side of the fabric other people will see.

Inside. The side of the fabric other people won't see—unless you wear the sweater inside-out.

Right hand knitters. Those who hold the yarn in their right hand.

Left hand knitters. Those who hold the yarn in their left hand.

Round knitters. Those who are working in rounds on a circular needle, or four, or more, double-points.

Flat knitters. Those who are working in rows on a circular needle, or two needles.

Seamline. This is not a seamline to be sewn, but an identification point for the right and left sides of the sweater body, for the raglan decreases in the yoke, and for the increases on the inner side of the sleeves.

One round. Once around the needle, or needles, from a starting point back to it.

One row. Once across the needle.

Outside round, or row. As you work, the outside of the sweater faces you.

Inside round, or row. As you work the inside of the sweater faces you.

Straight round, or row. A round, or row, without increases or decreases.

Decrease round, or row. A round, or row, with decreases.

Increase round, or row. A round, or row, with increases.

Plain round, or row. As opposed to one with pattern.

Pattern round, or row. As opposed to one that's plain.

Work. Keep on with whatever you are doing.

Stop. Stop working at a specified point, and go off and do something else.

Secure. Break the yarn; take the end to the inside; knot by taking the yarn under a handy stitch to form a loop and pulling the end through the loop.

Knit into. Knit under both strands of the chain selvedge to produce a stitch.

Unknit. Undo the stitches on the right hand needle, and put them back on the left needle.

Check point. To thine own gauge be true.

Decision point. Do you want a V neck, or don't you?

To the underarm. Assumes the position of 2″ below the actual body underarm.

The Basic Sweater. *K2, P2 ribbing, semi sleeves, seamline B and crew neck.*

THE BASIC SWEATER
adapted by the author from an original by Elizabeth Zimmermann

The Gauge Sample

Select your yarn. Take it to your needles. (For your first sweater, any medium weight yarn is best.) Work a gauge sample on a range of needles appropriate to the yarn, or inappropriate, for a special effect. Suggestions only:

Fine yarn—   #1 through #4.
Medium yarn—#4 through #8.
Heavy yarn—   #8 through #10½.

Note: A purl row is worked on the outside of the fabric sample to serve as a dividing line between needle sizes. As the needle size used at the final stitches-to-the-inch count is the body size needle for the sweater proper, you MUST know what size needle you used in that section. Don't trust your memory to keep track of the needle sizes. Jot the sizes down, in order, on a hang tag, or, for a built in record, work a corresponding number of purl stitches into a corner of the 3″ area. Separate the purl stitches with a few knits rather than working them side by side; it's quicker to count them. If you know immediately that a particular size needle is not producing the fabric you want, of course don't bother with the full 3 inches.

METHOD:

- Cast on 30 stitches.
- Work 6 rows of garter stitch.
- *Work 3'' of stockinette stitch, or your selected pattern.
- Stop after a purl row.
- Change to the next size needle, and purl a row.*
- Repeat * to * until you, the yarn, and the fabric are content.
- To end: work 6 rows of garter stitch. Cast-off.
- Or: keep the stitches on the needle for an on-going sample.

The Counting of the Stitches to the Inch

METHOD: Place the gauge sample flat on a table, not on your lap. Zero in on the area where the fabric looks and feels its best to you, **and** where it was comfortable for you to knit! For this measuring operation, a stitch gauge is best. Press its opening onto the sample, and with your finger carefully count the number of stitches within. Repeat in one or two more spots for accuracy. Do not ignore any half or quarter stitches in this count. Then divide the number of counted stitches by the length of the opening; most are 2''. The answer is your number of stitches to the inch. Before entering this number on *Gauge Page,* double-check the count: measure the width of the sample. Its width in inches should equal the gauge over 30 stitches. For example: with a gauge of 5 stitches to the inch, 30 stitches should produce a fabric sample 6'' wide. Would that for all the math was this simple, but you do relish a challenge, don't you?

If the stitches of a sample worked with handspun or novelty yarn are too ill-defined to count individually, you will have to average the stitches to the inch. In this case, measure the width of the sample and divide the number of inches into 30 stitches. For example: if the fabric measures 6'', divide 30 stitches by 6. The gauge is 5 stitches to the inch.

Enter the number of stitches to the inch on *Gauge Page* along with the corresponding needle size.

The Gauge Sample. *To count the number of stitches-to-the-inch, center the opening of a stitch and needle gauge over the section of the sample where the fabric looks and feels its best to you,* and *where it was comfortable for you to knit. Carefully, with your finger, count the stitches inside the opening and divide the number of stitches by the length of the opening to achieve your stitches-to-the-inch count.*

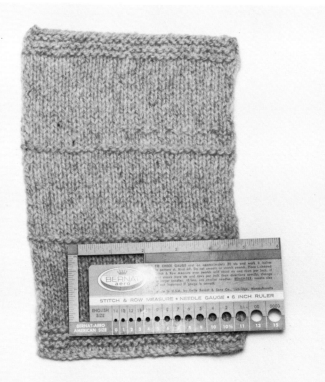

The Sweater Measurement

The fit of a sweater is indeed the most personal of matters. Some who measure a 34 are happy in a 32, where another might prefer a 40. For this reason, a body measurement is useless; it tells you nothing. Instead, measure your favorite fitting sweater. This is your only assurance that your new creation will fit "as you like it." But, before you go grabbing for any old sweater, herewith a few words of warning.

The sweater you measure must be of a similar weight yarn to the one you are to knit. It may surprise you to find that all your sweaters are not the same size; though you remain constant, they don't. The diameter of the yarn is the difference. A sweater of a heavy yarn has a wider outside measurement than a sweater of fine yarn. This is because of the sheer bulk of the yarn itself, and you must take this bulk into account. Inside, where you are, the sweater is smaller, but you must knit to the outside measurement. No more will you be knitting your sweaters all to one size. A size 36 sweater in a fine yarn may be perfect, but in a heavy yarn, too tight. So, be sure to measure a similar weight sweater. If you don't have a sweater close to your intended yarn, run to the nearest store with a tape measure.

For it matters not whether you measure a handknit, or a machinemade. And in the case of the latter, don't jump to conclusions. Though a commercial sweater may have a label that clearly states it is a certain size, don't trust your sweater's fate to others. Measure it yourself with a tape.

The Sweater Measurement. *In order that your new creation will fit "as you like it", measure your favorite fitting sweater of a similar weight yarn from underarm to underarm and double the number of inches.*

Take the sweater's measurement with the sweater smoothed on a flat surface, not on your body. Measure it from underarm to underarm, and don't forget to double the number of inches; the sweater does have another side.

Enter the sweater measurement on *Gauge Page.*

Now, the figuring begins. But, first, a round of applause for Elizabeth Zimmermann. That you are able to turn two simple measurements into a sweater of any size on your own is due to her EPS, otherwise known as Elizabeth's Percentage System. With her very kind permission, her EPS is presented here for you in the form of *Gauge Page.* Once you multiply your "stitches to the inch" by the inches around your sweater, you will be in proud possession of your Key Number and on the road to knitting on your own. Thank you, Elizabeth.

The Key Number of Stitches

METHOD: Multiply the number of stitches to the inch by the number of inches required for your sweater. The answer is your Key Number of stitches. The ultimate shape of the sweater depends on this number and the percentages derived from it. Complete your arithmetic, and check it for accuracy. In order to emphasize the importance of one-half, or one-quarter of a stitch per inch, and to point out how quickly these fractions disappear:

Gauge—	5 stitches	5 1/4 stitches	5 1/2 stitches
Sweater—	36 inches	36 inches	36 inches
Key #—	180 stitches	189 stitches	198 stitches

Figuring—	36	36	36
	× 5	× 5 1/4	× 5 1/2
	180	9	18
		180	180
		189	198

THE GAUGE PAGE

Gauge   = _____ stitches to the inch. (#____ needle)

Sweater Measurement = _____ inches around.

Body
Stitches × Inches   = _____ KEY NUMBER OF STITCHES.

Body Ribbing

          10% of KEY #   = _____.
Cast-on   = KEY # minus 10%   = _____. (#____ needle.)

Sleeves
Cuff-Ribbing   = 20% of KEY #   = _____.

Upperarm   = 33⅓ % of KEY # + 1 inch   = _____.

Increase   = upperarm minus cuff   = _____.

Underarm   = 8% of KEY #   = _____.

Figuring—

Sweater Style

Yarn Type

Finished Weight of Garment _____ ounces or grams.

The Body

The Body Ribbing. The body ribbing is worked on the Key Number of Stitches minus 10%.

For example—

Key # = 180 stitches	180	180
	× .10	– 18
10% of 180 = 18	18.00	162
180 minus 18 = 162		

Therefore, the number of stitches to cast on for the ribbing is 162. However, this number may have to be adjusted to accommodate the multiple of your selected ribbing pattern. For instance, if you want to work a K2, P2 ribbing, the number must be divisible by 4. 162 isn't, so it must be changed to 160 or 164. Up or down is up to you.

METHOD: Using a 24″ circular needle, *two sizes smaller* than the body size needle, cast on your ribbing number of stitches. Select a ribbing pattern with its pull-in tendencies in mind.

- Work the ribbing to within 1 round of the desired depth.
- On the last round of ribbing, increase the number of stitches by 10%—or more, or less, if you adjusted the ribbing number of stitches. Space these increases evenly throughout the round.
- *Stop* at the right seamline—above the tail of the slip knot. Count the number of stitches on the needle to be certain you have increased to the Key Number for the body of the sweater. If you are going to work a pattern into the body be certain that the number of stitches on the needle is a correct multiple.

The Body. The body is worked on your Key Number of stitches on the 24″ **body** size needle. To change from the ribbing size needle to the body needle simply work from one to the other.

METHOD: With the outside of the sweater facing you, tuck the right end of the ribbing needle down into your work. With the body size needle in your right hand insert the tip of it into the first stitch on the ribbing size needle in your left hand.

- Work one round.
- *Stop* at the right seamline. The ribbing needle is now empty. Before starting the next round, slip a marker on the right needle. ***This marker identifies the right seamline when the sweater is on you.*** It is the starting point of all rounds.
- As you work the next round, count the stitches. At the halfway point put a marker on the needle to identify the left seamline. Though you may not use these markers in a plain sweater until you reach the underarm, they will be there for reference and provide a feeling of security.
- Work round and round until your sweater measures about 3″ above the ribbing.
- *Stop* at the right seamline.

Check-point: At this point your sweater may look too small. Keep in mind the three legitimate reasons for its appearance:
1. It is on a 24" needle.
2. The ribbing has been worked on a needle two sizes smaller, and on 10% fewer stitches.
3. You have worked a decent ribbing with good pull-in tendencies.

Though the sweater may look too small at Check Point—3" above the ribbing—it will be the correct size when it gets where its going, which is to the underarm, if your gauge is correct.

Now, for the illegitimate reason, and why you must check the fit at this point:

Your gauge sample was worked back and forth on two needles. Once you start zipping around on a circular needle your tension could change; a few knitters tighten up, a few loosen up. So, to check your gauge and to check the fit, slip (as if to purl) approximately half the stitches onto the empty ribbing needle. This move will allow your sweater to open up to its full width. With the sweater thus released from the confines of the 24" needle, count the number of stitches to the inch—again, over more than one inch, and in two or three spots.

If all is in order as far as gauge is concerned, slip what there is of the sweater onto your body. Check the width of the ribbing in the desired position, and then hike the body part of the sweater up.

If the fit is satisfactory, put the stitches back on the body size needle and continue working.

Check-point. *With half its body stitches slipped onto a spare 24" circular needle, what there is of the sweater is ready for a gauge check and a try-on. Note: to hold the markers on the needle, work one stitch beyond them, and to hold the stitches on the needle for the try-on, tightly wrap elastics around their individual ends.*

If you detect a change in gauge, *start again.* Use the gauge achieved on round needles for setting up a new *Gauge Page.* Take note of the words ''start again''; a more pleasant approach than rip out, and a more exact assessment of the situation. The thought, and the job, of ripping is demoralizing; it can ruin an otherwise beautiful day. In addition, it is not wise—not all at once anyway. For how are you to know if the second attempt is an improvement over the first if the first is gone? The psychological and sensible solution is to knit as you rip. And, you are in a perfect position to do so starting as you are with a ribbing. Ribbings are the best home for ripped yarn as worked on smaller needles than the body proper, any loss of bulk is less noticeable.

So, to start again, pull the needle, break the yarn and place the reject beside you. Then rip a round, and rib a round. When the new ribbing is complete, check its new size with what is left of the reject. In the same manner, use the remainder of the original ribbing for ribbing the sleeves and the neck. Before you know it, the distasteful task of ripping is done, and the reject is gone; the best part is that you never had to look at a horrid ball of kinky yarn.

Apply the same philosophy to other situations. Don't rip. Wait until you must use the yarn, and aim for ribbings. To change in mid-sweater from new yarn to used might be detectable. However, if necessary, give it a try. The alternative is to restore the yarn's fullness by washing. But, in that case, you may be committed to washing all the yarn for the project; washing only the ripped yarn could make a bad situation worse.

Or, don't rip at all. You have the ready-made start of another sweater, or, if small enough, a cap or a turtle-to-go. If the reject ribbing was to be a cardigan, bind it off for a matching scarf. Lastly, many small errors are easily corrected with a crochet hook; dropped stitches, forgotten decreases, and reversed stitches—knits that should be purls, or vice versa, are instances that may not require ripping. Try anything first. Treat ripping as a last resort. And remember, everything hand-done is entitled to one tiny mistake.

Now, back to the business at hand. If you had to start again, knit faster to catch up.

As you work to the underarm, consider the following Decision Points:

> ***Decision point for short rows***—3″ above the ribbing.
> ***Decision point for sweatshirt pocket***—5″ or 6″ above the ribbing for an adult; 3″ or 4″ for a child.

Stripes, patterns, designs or other decorations may be added anywhere you like. For a pattern, or a design, select one with a multiple that works in with a minimal change to your Key Number of stitches. An adjustment of one or two stitches is tolerable—any more than that would affect the size of the sweater. See Ideas and Patterns, p. 102.

- Work the body until you are about 2″ shy of your actual underarm.
- ***Stop*** at the right seam line.
  Once more, to be absolutely certain of the correct body length, slip half the stitches onto another needle, and try on the body. With the ribbing where you want it, check the position of the top of the body in relation to the underarm. Then slip the stitches back on the body needle. Be sure they are on the ***body*** needle. If you must adjust, up or down, do so, but be absolutely sure that when you stop you,
- ***Stop at the right seamline.*** Do not break the body yarn. Start the sleeve with a new ball.

The Sleeve

The Sleeve Ribbing. The sleeve ribbing is worked on 20% of the Key Number of Stitches.

For example—	Figuring—	
Key # = 180 stitches		180
		× .20
20% of 180 = 36		36.00

Therefore, the number of stitches to cast on for the sleeve ribbing is 36. If the number must be adjusted to work your ribbing pattern, consider the size of your wrist. By now you must know whether it is a little smaller, or larger, than "normal." Adjust the number up or down accordingly.

The ribbing is worked on four double-pointed ribbing size needles.

METHOD: Cast your ribbing number of stitches all onto *one* needle *loosely*.

- Divide the stitches onto three needles by slipping them (as if to purl) from the one to the other two. Starting with the last cast-on stitch, slip 1/3 of the stitches onto an empty needle. Then slip the next third onto another empty needle. Each needle does not have to have an exact number of stitches; your tension will be better if each needle starts with a knit stitch as opposed to a purl.
- Hold the needle with the tail in your left hand.
- Hold the needle with the last cast-on stitch and the working yarn in your right hand.
- Be certain all the stitches are straight on the needle with their bottoms under the needle.
- Carefully transfer all three needles to your left hand and, with the fourth needle in your right hand, insert the tip of it into the slip knot stitch, and work the stitches from the first needle in ribbing pattern onto the fourth needle.
- Insert the now-empty first needle into the first stitch on the second needle, and continuing in ribbing pattern, work the stitches from the second needle onto the first. Insert the now-empty second needle into the first stitch on the third needle, and continuing in ribbing pattern, work the stitches from the third needle onto the second. You are now back where you started, and the empty third needle starts the next round.
- Continue rotating needles as they empty. Be sure your work is on three needles at all times. The sleeve ribbing grows **toward** you, with the tail of the slip knot marking the seamline.
- Work the sleeve ribbing to desired depth for wearing as is, or longer, if it is to be folded back.

• **Stop** at the seam line knowing there is one last round of ribbing to be worked.

> ***Decision point for sleeve style:*** For your first sweater, select one of the following three sleeve styles. After that, you may be as fancy as you wish as long as you end up at the upperarm with one-third (33⅓%) plus an inch's worth of stitches.

The upperarm is 33⅓%, or one-third of the Key Number of stitches plus one inch's worth of stitches.

For example— Figuring—

$$3 \overline{\smash{\big)}\ 180} \quad = 60$$

Key # = 180 stitches
33⅓% of 180 = 60
60 + 1 inch = 65

After determining the number of stitches needed at the upperarm, subtract the number of stitches you already have on the needle for the ribbing.

For example—   Figuring—
Upperarm = 66 (round off) stitches   66
Ribbing = 36   − 36
Increase = 30   30

Therefore, the number of stitches to be increased somewhere, somehow, as you work your way up the sleeve is 30.

METHOD:

The Full Sleeve. Increase all the stitches you need to achieve the upper arm total in the last round of ribbing, spacing them evenly.

The Semi Sleeve. Increase one-half (or more, or less) of the stitches you need for your upperarm total in the last round of ribbing; increase the other half (or more, or less) by pairs between the elbow and the upperarm. The "more or less" is noted to call your attention to the fact that the number of stitches to be increased does not have to be divided exactly in half. To simplify the math, and make the increases more convenient, split the number off-center. To use the example for an example:

> The number of stitches to increase is 30. The number of stitches already on the needle for the ribbing is 36. Rather than split the number of stitches to be increased into 15 and 15, split them into 18 and 12. That way you will increase into every other stitch on the ribbing needle, as 18 is half of 36; and the remaining 12 you will increase in 6 pairs of two's between the elbow and the upperarm.

The Fitted Sleeve. Increase one inch's worth of stitches in the last round of ribbing; increase the remainder, by pairs, starting one inch above the ribbing, and every inch thereafter. For the inch's worth of stitches, refer to your gauge. To use the example for an example:

Gauge is 5 to the inch. Round this off to 4 or 6, knowing your wrist. You would then be left with either 26 or 24 to increase by pairs as you work up the sleeve.
- Make a decision on sleeve style and work the last round of ribbing, increasing the appropriate number of stitches.

The Sleeve Proper. The sleeve is worked on four double-pointed body size needles, unless and until you have enough stitches to comfortably fit around a 16″ circular needle. (Even if you have selected the full sleeve and numberwise now have enough stitches to fit around the 16″ needle, the stitches have not yet had a chance to blossom to their full width.)

Therefore, one by one, as you work the next round, change from the four ribbing size double-pointed needles to four body size double-pointed needles.

If you are working the fitted sleeve, the paired increases are made at the seam line. As the seam line is now between two needles, a marker would not stay put. So, on the next round, slip the stitches around on the needles and position the seam line in the center of one. This move also makes the increase track more visible.

Work the sleeve until you are about 2″ shy of your actual underarm. Try the sleeve on as you work with the ribbing folded up or down; however you intend to wear it.
- *Stop* at the seamline when the length is correct. Break the yarn, leaving a good yard and tuck it down into the sleeve. Work the other sleeve to match.

If you must use the same needles for the other sleeve, slip the stitches from the finished sleeve onto anything from which they may be worked—a good job for the plastic needles you now do not know what to do with. In any case, do not put the stitches of the finished sleeve onto a stitch holder, or on a scrap of yarn; that move will only slow down the joining round, and add an unnecessary step to the proceedings.

Joining the Sleeves and Body

The Preparation for Joining

The number of stitches for each underarm section of the body and the sleeves is 8% of the Key Number of stitches.

For example—   Figuring—
Key # = 180 stitches   180
                                         × .08
                                        ───────
.08 of 180 = 14   14.40

Therefore, the number of stitches to be left behind for the underarm grafting is 14. Disregard any figures beyond the decimal point, and round off to the nearest even number. Thread the Braidkin with a yard of scrap yarn.

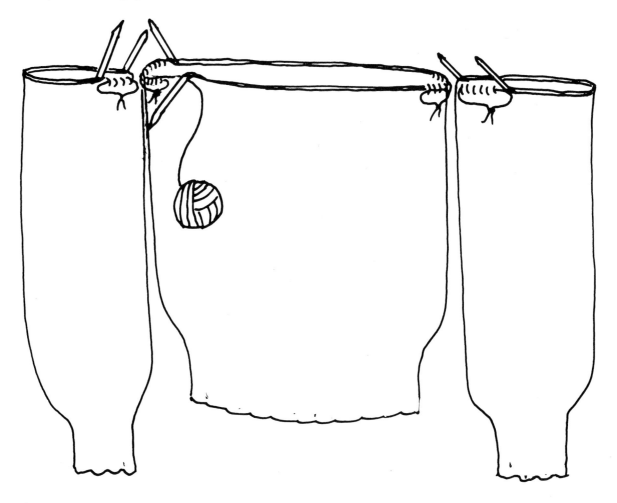

Sleeve Preparation.

METHOD: The seamline is the center of the underarm stitches; one-half are to the right, one-half are to the left. The sleeve knitting stopped at the seamline, and the sleeve yarn is in the center of the underarm stitches.

- Unknit the right half of the underarm stitches, which automatically transfers them to the left needle.
- Slip the underarm stitches (as if to purl) from the left needle onto the Braidkin. Pull the scrap yarn through the underarm stitches; break it and tie the ends loosely. The rest of the sleeve stitches remain on the knitting needle, or needles for the moment.
- Repeat on the other sleeve.

The Joining Round. *With the body and sleeves worked to the underarms, the sweater is ready to be joined together. One at a time, the sleeves are connected to the body; all the stitches are thus united on the body needle, except for the underarm stitches that hang by their scraps until they are grafted.*

Body Preparation: the Right Seamline

METHOD: The right seamline is the center of the underarm stitches; one-half are to the right, one-half are to the left. The body knitting stopped at the seamline and the body yarn is in the center of the underarm stitches.

- Unknit the right half of the underarm stitches, which automatically transfers them to the left needle.
- Slip the underarm stitches (as if to purl) from the left needle onto the Braidkin.
- Pull the scrap yarn through the stitches; break it and tie the ends loosely.

   In order that the underarm stitches at the left seamline are prepared for your arrival as you work the Joining Round, they also are to be put on a scrap. However—do not knit your way over to them. Just pick up your Braidkin and go to:

Body Preparation: the Left Seamline

METHOD: The left seamline is the center of the underarm stitches; one-half are to the right; one-half are to the left.

- Run the Braidkin with the scrap yarn through the underarm stitches.
- Break the yarn, and tie the ends loosely. The left underarm stitches stay on the yarn and on the needle for the moment.

   The three pieces of knitting are now prepared for the joining round.

The Joining Round

One at a time, the sleeves are to be joined to the body. All the body and sleeve stitches will end up on the body needle *except* for the underarm stitches. They will hang by their scraps until the sweater is done and then be grafted together. Think sewing. You're not going to; just think it.

METHOD: Pick up the body.

- Hold it just as you would to continue knitting with the outside facing you and the right seamline to your left.
- Tuck the end of the body needle that is now at the back out of the way. At the moment it is separated from its mate by the underarm stitches, but in just a minute they will be together again clicking away in perfect harmony. Now,
- Pick up a sleeve. Either one. They are both the same—unless you have done something strange to one, such as a monogram, or an asymmetrical design, and therefore have a particular arm in mind.
- Holding the sleeve outside the body at the right underarm, match the underarm stitches of the sleeve to the underarm stitches of the body.
- *With the body needle and body yarn in your right hand and the sleeve needle in your left hand, insert the tip of the body needle into the first stitch on the sleeve needle. (This first stitch on the sleeve needle is the first stitch to the left of the underarm stitches.) Work the sleeve stitches from the sleeve needle, or needles, onto the body needle. Find the left end of the body needle.*

- Using the body needles, work across the back of the sweater until you come to the left underarm stitches that are on the needle as well as the scrap.
- Remove the left needle from these stitches. Let them hang loose on their scrap.
- Pick up the other sleeve.
- Hold it outside the body at the left underarm, matching the underarm stitches of the sleeve to the underarm stitches of the body.
- Repeat * to *.
- Using the body needles, work across the front of the sweater.
- *Stop* where you started the joining round.

> ***Important—two must do's—***
>> 1. Put a large safety pin somewhere in the sweater near this point to quickly identify the front of the sweater.
>> 2. Put a marker (green for go, if you have one) on the needle between the body stitch and the first sleeve stitch.

This marker will forevermore be referred to as the marker at the **right front seamline.** The raglan seamline decreases, the neckline set-ups, and anything else in the yoke of the sweater depend on it as a reference point.

The Marker Round

Work the next round, putting markers at the other 3 points where the sleeves join the body. If you are working in a pattern, check to be sure it joined correctly. If you must adjust, do so near the joining points on this round.

Stop, Read, Rejoice. Feed the cat. Walk the dog, Your knitting is all* together. *You are on the home stretch.

You are now approaching the yoke of the sweater. The yoke is defined as the upper part of the sweater from the joining round to the neck ribbing. It develops four raglan seamlines as you decrease at the four marked joining points, and somewhere along the way it also develops a neckline. The former remains consistent for any sweater; the latter varies as to its starting point and set-up depending on the style.

The basic sweater takes you through the Crew Neck. By so doing, come the next sweater, you will have the decreases at the raglan seamlines down pat and can concentrate on constructing a different neckline.

- Work around all the stitches for 1½″.
- *Stop* at the right front seamline. ***Read.***

The Raglan Decreases

The raglan decreases start 1½″ above the joining round, which is where are. Make a quick check of the following: Count to be sure the front stitches equal the back stitches. Count to be sure the sleeve stitches equal each other. (The sleeve stitches are not equal to the back and front stitches.) If you find an error, mark the section it is in, and correct it on the next round by knitting two together near a joining point.

Refer to raglan seamline decreases in the sampler, and refresh your memory as to their characteristics. Select A, B, B-Reverse, C, D, or E. The decrease rounds start at the marker at the right front seamline, actually 2 or 3 stitches before this marker depending on the decrease you have chosen.

To shape the yoke, you will work a paired decrease at each of the raglan seamline markers *every fourth round,* three times, and then *every other round* until the sleeves are gone. Though the neck shaping starts before the sleeves are gone, it in no way interferes with this rate of decrease at the raglan seamlines. To keep track of your first few decrease rounds, check off the following chart as you work up the yoke from the joining round. The chart is simply to get you started in proper order. If you find it helpful, continue it on a scrap of paper, or in the book itself—feel free to scratch. However, don't go racing all the way to the top of the sweater. Once a few decrease rounds have been worked, and you are accustomed to them, take a break and check in on the Decision Point for the Crew Neck. If you go too far, you'll have to rip back.

RAGLAN DECREASE CHART

To start the yoke and the raglan seam line decreases, follow this chart and check off the rounds as you work the yoke from the joining round *up.*

_____ straight
_____ decrease
_____ straight
_____ decrease
_____ straight
_____ decrease
_____ straight
_____ straight
_____ straight
_____ decrease
_____ straight
_____ straight
_____ straight
_____ decrease
_____ straight
_____ straight
_____ straight
_____ decrease ◄ **you are here**
___✔___ 1 ½ straight inches
___✔___ marker round
___✔___ joining round

The Crew Neck

Decision Point: * The Crew Neck Shaping starts when 20 or 21 stitches remain to be decreased on each sleeve. This count of the number of stitches remaining to be decreased must be done correctly; it is vital to the neckline shaping. ***Do not count between the markers.*** To do so would be to include the raglan seam line stitches with the sleeve stitches. The raglan seam line stitches, two, three, or four of them, sit, one or two on one side of the marker and one or two on the other. ***These seam line stitches are unto themselves, and are not counted anywhere for anything.*** By now, they should be very visible. Hold them out of the way, and count *only* the number of stitches *between* the seam lines. ***Take this count on a straight round.*** When counting the number of stitches in the front of the sweater, to set up the neckline shaping, follow suit. ***Do not count from the marker.*** Do not include any seam line stitches in the count. Count from the seam line.

Set up: Work until 20 or 21 stitches remain to be decreased on each sleeve. (If the sleeve had an even number of stitches as you started to decrease, you will have 20. If the sleeve had an uneven number of stitches as you started to decrease, you will have 21.)

METHOD:
- ***Stop*** at the right front seam line after a ***straight*** round.
- Thread a Braidkin with a scrap of yarn.
- Run the scrap through all the front stitches *except for 14 on* each side next to the sleeves. Tie the scrap loosely.
- These center front stitches remain on the scrap and on the needle for the moment.
- Work a decrease round until you come to the center stitches.
- Remove the needle from these stitches.
- ***Stop. Read.***

The center front stitches are to remain behind hanging on the scrap until the neck shaping is complete. Because they have interrupted your immediate round of knitting, you were unable to complete a full round back to the right front seam line. If it bothers you or your pattern that the stitches in the section to the left of the center front stitches will be minus a row of work in the final accounting, you may need to work them separately, just this once. This step is known as the Catch-Up Row. It can usually be omitted in a one color sweater without a pattern. For those of you who need it:

The Catch-Up Row: With the outside facing, and with a separate length of yarn, and with a double-pointed body size needle in your right hand, work the unworked stitches from the right side neck ***to*** the decrease at the right front seam line. (Do ***not*** work a decrease

---

*This Decision Point assumes you are working with a medium or heavy weight yarn. If you are using a fine yarn, see The Mathematics of the Crew Neck Shaping, p. 98.

here—you did at the start of the round.) Slip the caught-up stitches back on the body needle. The round is now complete. Return to the body yarn.

Working the neck back and forth. You will now be working back and forth on the needle. If you are working in a pattern, you may have to reverse your knits and purls on the inside rows. You will no longer be working in rounds that start at the right front seamline. You will be working in rows that start with the first stitches on the needle at the right and left side neck edges. This in no way affects your decreases at the raglan seamlines. If anything, it makes it easier to keep track of your decrease rounds vs. your straight rounds:

The *outside* rows are the decrease rows.

The *inside* rows are the straight rows.

From now on, start all rows with a slip stitch for a chain selvedge:

Outside rows—slip as if to purl, yarn in back.

Inside rows—slip as if to purl, yarn in front.

METHOD:

- *Turn your work.* With the inside facing you, and with the right end of the body needle in your right hand, ***work the inside row.***
- *On the next 4 outside rows only,* decrease 1 stitch at the neck edges *and* continue to decrease at the raglan seamlines: Start and end these next 4 outside rows: Slip 1, K2tog., *work* to the last 3 stitches, SSK, K1.
- *Then,* continue the decreases at the raglan seamlines **only** until the seamlines come together and the sleeve is gone.
- *Stop* at the end of an outside row.

The Crew Neck—before its ribbing. *The Crew Neck is pictured here "in the rough". It started to develop its shape when 20 stitches remained to be decreased on the sleeve, and all the front stitches were put on a scrap except for 14 on each side next to the sleeves. These center front stitches were left behind while the sides of the Crew Neck were shaped (note the chain selvedge), and, at the same time, the raglan seam line decreasing continued until the sleeves were gone; a series of events that allowed the back of the neck to keep rising.*

Now, the neck is ready for its ribbing. As you can see, work stopped at the end of an outside row. At this point a 16" circular ribbing size needle is called into service, and starting at the shoulder with the body yarn, it first knits up and establishes the number of stitches for the neck ribbing. Note how few there are to knit up; most are already in existence on the scrap and body needle. Then, the ribbing is started in your chosen pattern.

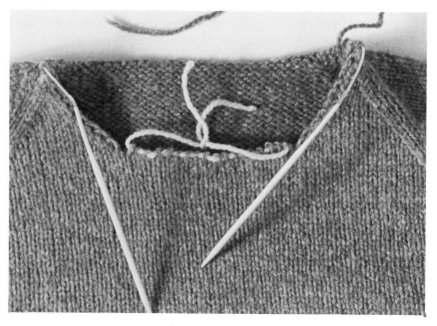

The Neck Ribbing

Note—The left side neck is the left side neck when the sweater is on you.

The right side neck is the right side neck when the sweater is on you.

METHOD: Using a 16″ circular ribbing size needle in your right hand:

- Knit into the left side neck chain selvedge,
- Knit the stitches on the scrap (slip them onto a double-point),
- Knit into the right side neck chain selvedge, and,
- Knit the back neck stitches from the body needle. ***Stop.***
- Count the number of stitches on the needle. If the number must be adjusted for the ribbing pattern, do so in the first round of ribbing near a raglan seamline.
- Put a marker on the right needle and work the ribbing pattern loosely for an inch. Neck ribbing should not pull-in. The purl stitches are open and visible, not hidden as in the ribbing on the body or the sleeves.
- Cast off in ribbing, ***loosely.***

The Underarm Opening

METHOD:

- Slip a double-pointed needle through the body stitches at the left underarm. Remove the scrap.
- Slip a double-pointed needle through the sleeve stitches at the left underarm. Remove the scrap.
- Now, insert the tip of *each* end of *each* needle into the sweater itself and pick up the stitch adjacent to the opening.

The underarm graft—getting ready. *Needles are inserted through underarm and body stitches,* **plus** *one sweater stitch at each end of the opening.*

- Reach into the sleeve and pull out the reserved yard of yarn.
- Thread the end through the Braidkin. With the outside of the sweater facing you, and the opening in a horizontal position, the

attached yarn should be at the right end of the opening. Notice that the yarn is in the center of the right side of the opening. To begin grafting it must be coming from the first stitch on the back needle. The back needle is the needle furthest away from you. The front needle is the needle nearest you. To position the yarn correctly, a preliminary step is necessary:

- Slip the Braidkin through the first stitch on the right end of the back needle as if to knit; pull the yarn through the stitch leaving the stitch on the needle.
- The yarn is now where it should be to begin grafting.

Refer to Grafting in the sampler, p. 42. When the grafting row is complete, adjust the new stitches to the tension of the sweater fabric. Grafting the one extra stitch from the sweater itself at each end of each needle tends to minimize any possible hole at the corners of the opening. However, if you have been left with one, treat it gently. Using the yarn in the Braidkin, or a separate length with a crochet hook, circle around the hole and ease it out of existence. The less done the better. Repeat the grafting process at the right underarm opening. Finis. Wear Proudly.

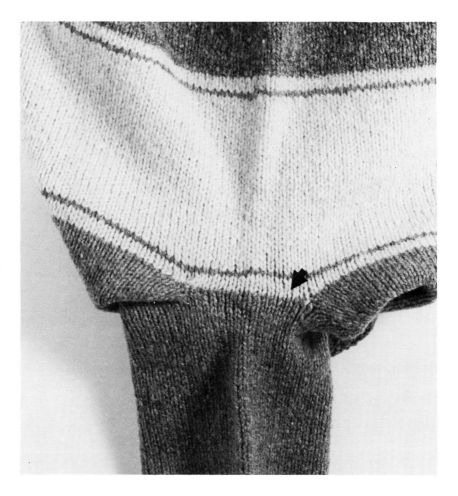

The Underarm Grafting— completed. *Kitchener Stitch produces an invisible "seam" at the underarm, even when the two sections to be grafted—the body underarm stitches and the sleeve underarm stitches—are of different colors. However, more important than its looks, is its comfort, for the "seam" has the same tension and give as the sweater fabric.*

The Yoke

The mathematics of the yoke shaping is not mandatory reading, unless you are interested in the whys and wherefores of what you have just accomplished. You should, however, acquaint yourself with it if you intend to add an allover precision-type stripe, pattern, or design; for in that case, you must know the number of rounds from the joining to the neck ribbing.

The mathematics of the yoke shaping. The number of rounds in the yoke (from the joining to the neck ribbing), approximately equals the number of stitches on one sleeve after the joining round, for the sleeve is decreased until it is gone at the approximate rate of 2 stitches every other round. This is the equivalent of 1 stitch to 1 round. Therefore:

1 sleeve stitch equals 1 round, and
_____ sleeve stitches equal _____ rounds.

To figure the number of rounds in the yoke exactly, you must take into consideration the number of rounds in the straight 1½ "; the number of additional straight rounds when you are decreasing every fourth round rather than every other round; and the number of stitches lost to the seamline itself. Therefore:

The stitches on one sleeve plus the number of additional straight rounds equal _____.
Subtract the number of stitches lost to the seamline _____.
The number of rounds in the yoke then equals _____.

For those not attuned to slide rule math, hit-or-miss stripes will liven up the yoke with less mental effort. Though worked in the round, stripes take a right angle turn at the raglan seamlines— a departure from the expected and a fillip for geometric souls. Always change from one color to the next at the right front seamline. If you happen to change on a decrease round, work the first half of the decrease in the new color.

A small band of two color knitting is almost as carefree an addition as stripes. A good guess will more than likely land it in a logical position. However, limit the two color work to a 3, 4 or 5 round design. To keep its multiple intact, you may interrupt the normal sequence of raglan decreases, but you should work a decrease round immediately before, and immediately after the pattern rounds. Be aware that by omitting a decrease round or two, the yoke will be a few rounds deeper. Pre-planned, you could shorten up on the "decrease, three straight" sequence to compensate. And, of course, before you start, count all the stitches to be certain you have the correct multiple.

To work a two color pattern throughout a raglan yoke means to bite the bullet and accept the fact that the pattern will be cut off at the pass, so to speak, as you work the decreases at the raglan seamlines. If you're not the type for this sort of imprecision, you'd best try to find a pattern for a Fair Isle yoke that is an approximate multiple of whatever you have on the needle for stitches after the joining round. The decreases for a Fair Isle yoke are built into the pattern and scattered throughout the yoke; they are not concentrated in four seamlines. To lessen the customary "rolling folds" in the front of a Fair Isle, select a pattern with at least five or six decrease rounds, or, if you're not allergic to two color knitting in the flat, work the yoke with a placket neck; the slash alleviates the fitting problem.

To convert a raglan yoke to a Fair Isle Yoke, you may need to know the total number of stitches that would be decreased in the raglan for a comparison. Therefore:

The total number of stitches decreased in the raglan yoke is based on the number of decrease rounds which is based on the number of sleeve stitches. The sleeve is decreased by 2 stitches every decrease round. Therefore:

The number of sleeve stitches _____ divided by 2 _____ equals the number of decrease rounds.

In each decrease round, two stitches are decreased at each of the four seamlines for a total of eight stitches every decrease round. Therefore:

The number of decrease rounds _____ times 8 _____ equals the total number of stitches decreased in the yoke.

And, for what it's worth, you are approximately decreasing 4 stitches every round above the straight 1½″.

The mathematics of the neck shaping. The mathematics of the neck shaping is mandatory reading. It explains the reasoning of the Crew Neck shaping which is the basis for the U-Neck, the Slit Neck, the Placket Neck and the Cardigan, as well as adjustments for neckline depth and for yarn diameter.

The set-up and the decreasing for every neckline depends on the number of stitches remaining to be decreased on the sleeve; for when the sleeve is gone, the neckline must be complete. To better understand this close relationship of sleeve to neckline, concentrate on the right front seamline of your Crew Neck for a moment.

As a paired decrease was worked at this seamline, one of the front stitches and one of the sleeve stitches were devoured. Keep in mind that only one half of the sleeve stitches were decreased at the right front seamline; the other half were decreased at the back seamline. To grasp the principle of the Crew Neck shaping, you need only consider the half that is decreased on the right front seamline; the back takes care of itself.

The Crew Neck shaping started when 20 stitches remained to be decreased on the sleeve. Of the 20 stitches, 10, or one-half were decreased at the right front seamline. In order to work a paired decrease at this seamline, 10 of the front stitches had to be there on the needle, available as partners. To round the corner for the Crew Neck required 4 stitches. As 10 plus 4 equals 14, you may now see why and from where cometh:

> "When 20 stitches remain to be decreased on each sleeve, run a scrap yarn through all the front stitches except for 14 on each side next to the sleeves."

Matched stitch for stitch, the 10 of the sleeve disappeared with the 10 of the front, and the 4 vanished at the neck edge. Thus, when the sleeve was gone, the neck was complete.

On that same basis, you may start the Crew Neck wherever you wish. If 20 seemed too high in a medium weight yarn, start the set-up when 26 stitches remain to be decreased on the sleeve. One-half of 26 is 13, so 13 sleeve stitches are to be decreased at the right front seamline. Therefore, leave 13 plus 4, or 17 on the needle at each side next to the sleeve, and put the rest on a scrap. The Crew Neck shaping in a fine yarn should begin back when 30 stitches remain to be decreased on the sleeve, for the stitches are smaller and the rounds to the inch are less. In that case, one-half of 30 being 15, you would leave 15 plus 4, or 19 stitches on the needle at each side next to the sleeves, and put the rest on a scrap. In fact, in a fine yarn, it might take 6 stitches to round the corner; if so, leave 15 plus 6, or 21 stitches on the needle at each side next to the sleeves, and work 6 decreases at the neck edge.

To sum up: you may start the Crew Neck shaping wherever you wish; if it's low enough, it will become the U-Neck. The formula is: count the number of stitches remaining to be decreased on one sleeve, divide by 2, and add 4. The answer is the number of stitches to leave on the needle at each side front next to the sleeves; put the remaining center stitches on a scrap.

Minor Adjustments

The Basic Sweater is constructed on principles and percentages to fit the average figure. The following adjustments may be made if necessary:

The sleeves and/or the body may be lengthened or shortened by working more, or fewer, rounds to the underarm. No suggested lengths were given for these measures, as individuals and sweater styles vary so. A short-waisted knitter might find an 11″ body is perfect; but that would never do for someone taller. Take advantage of the fact that the construction is such that the sweater pieces may be tried on as you work. To knit a sweater for someone other than yourself, it would be necessary to know the body length and sleeve length as well as the sweater measurement itself at the underarm. Again, take these measurements from the recipient's favorite fitting sweater if the body isn't handy for a fitting.

The yoke may be made deeper by decreasing every fourth round a few more times than prescribed. For the Crew Neck style, another alternative would be to decrease every third round all the way to the top.

For a shorter yoke, cut down on the number of times you decrease every fourth round. However, don't cut it out entirely. Work the first decrease round followed by three straight rounds at least once. To start decreasing every other round immediately brings the seamlines together too rapidly and the fabric will pucker at the base of the seamline.

The sleeves and/or the shoulders may be made wider by adding two inch's worth of stitches to the 33% for the upperarm. The Crew Neck shaping would then start when you had 20 plus the additional stitches remaining to be decreased on each sleeve. Once the neck shaping is complete, and the 14 stitches at each side neck are worked, the sleeves will not be gone; the added stitches will remain between the seamlines for extra width.

To narrow the sleeve at the upperarm, do not add the prescribed inch's worth of stitches to the 33%. Keep trying on the sleeve as you work it. If it is wide enough without the added inch's worth of stitches, don't bother with them. Stop increasing when you reach the 33% figure.

The more sweaters you knit, the cannier you will become. Once you realize you are in control of your own sweater, you will gain the confidence to rely on your own good common sense; not only for fit, but for fashion. Experiment and adventure are yours for the knitting.

THE SWEATER VARIATIONS

The Basic Sweater is the point of departure for an endless number of variations. More versions of this simple, classic crew neck style are shown beginning on page 120.

Ideas

If not during, then certainly after the first sweater "on your own," you will find yourself translating ideas from everywhere into sweater designs. Jot them down, cut them out, or simply stash them in your subconscious for future reference. Just brushing the surface with a few ideas to add to yours:

1. Museums—where else for such an abundance of color and design? Study your best loved paintings for color ideas, and check the old textiles.

2. Your old or very old pattern books—stylewise, history has a way of repeating itself.

3. Current fashion magazines—or better yet, get your name on the right list and you'll be on the receiving end of the best in catalogs.

4. Other sweaters—in stores, or on your friends, neighbors, fellow travelers, co-workers, or complete strangers. When they ask you what you're doing up that close, just tell them: counting stitches.

5. Spinners—"think mink." Once off the farm, the wooly black fleece is as fine as anything in the fur department. Its rich, natural shadings are every bit as wondrous as those of an expensive skin. Check out the latest styles, and give your handspun the fur coat treatment. Or, if you can find it, spin mink!

6. Weavers—knit your weaving patterns.

7. Braiders—think color as for a rug; one in, one out.

8. Nature—a goldenrod sweater with a million pockets.

9. Your yarn—ideas of its own, perhaps. Pick it up and get started.

10. Last, but not least, the library—and, venture out of 746.43. Wander through the math, music, antique, and art design shelves. Forthwith a few examples:

Fibonacci Sequence.[*] Leonardo Fibonacci was a 13th century mathematician. When asked, "How many pairs of rabbits can be produced from a single pair in a year, if each pair begets a new pair every month, and each new pair reproduces from the second month on, and, no rabbit dies?" His answer works well in a sweater: **1** and **1** are **2**; 1 and 2 are **3**; 2 and 3 are **5**; 3 and 5 are **8**; 5 and 8 are **13**; 8 and 13 are **21**; 13 and 21 are **34**; etc., etc., etc. The sequence is arrived at by starting with 1 and 1 and continually adding the two previous numbers. In short: 1, 1, 2, 3, 5, 8, 13, 21, 34, and on, for as many rabbits as you'd care to knit. Work the sequence in two colors, or as many as will fit into a sweater. Work a purl round leaving the sequence in between as stockinette. Work the sequence in reverse for a yoke. For a more random stripe or sequence try:

[*]William Karush, *The Crescent Dictionary of Mathematics.*

[*]*Thank you, Connie Pearlstein for applying "Fibonacci" to the knitted fabric.*

Ringing the Changes.* The pealing of 5 church bells, tuned to the major scale and rung in succession, will add rhythm to a sweater. The first series of 5 bells ring in this order: (read the rows left to right from top to bottom.)

(start)	Color Translation—
1, 2, 3, 4, 5,	#1 bell—_____ color
2, 1, 4, 3, 5,	#2 bell—_____ color
2, 4, 1, 5, 3,	#3 bell—_____ color
4, 2, 5, 1, 3,	#4 bell—_____ color
4, 5, 2, 3, 1. (end)	#5 bell—_____ color

Select five colors, or even five yarns. Assign each one to a bell. Starting with the round above the ribbing, work one round of #1, two rounds of #2, three rounds of #3, four rounds of #4, five rounds of #5. That completes the first sequence (top row, reading left to right). Now start the second row which begins to mix the colors and/or yarns up a bit; work two rounds of #2; one round of #1; etc., etc. Complete the series and start again.

The number of bells that ring in a series can vary from five to twelve, and the number of changes possible with twelve bells (or twelve colors) is 479,001,600. That ought to keep you in striped sweaters forever.

And, while you're in a musical mood, why not knit your favorite song. On a scale of 1 to 8, you might complete a bar or two.

The Dedham Bunny.** An alternative to the overabundance of whales and alligators is the famous rabbit pattern of The Dedham Pottery Company. This distinct New England pottery dates from the late 1800's and was the creation of Hugh Robertson. The off-white rabbits in a cobalt blue border ran around plates, mugs, bowls, and pitchers. They are equally engaging running around sweaters in the same or reverse color treatment.

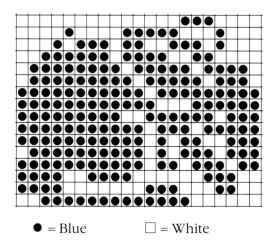

● = Blue   □ = White

The New Grove Dictionary of Music, Vol. 4, p. 134.
**Heinz, Edgar Kiewe, *History of Folk Cross-stitch,* p. 76.

Left: *V-Neck Cardigan with ribbed tie (p. 156); V-Neck in textured cotton yarn; (p. 129) Open Raglan (p. 145) with matching Beaded Rib scarf (p. 177).*

Right: *Handspun V-Neck with lacing (p. 129); handspun camel hair ''three V-neck'' vest; Crew Neck with purl stripes of handspun camel hair (p. 120); and Cardigan Vest (p. 167).*

Handspun Crew Neck with Candlelit Windows yoke pattern (p. 122); handspun Slit Neck sweater in reverse stockinette with laced neckline (p. 134); Mushroom Cap in natural handspun wool (p. 176).

Color Study Sources. Margaret Walch's book* is an arrangement of palettes, not only of famous artists and craftsmen, but of cultures and times. A glance through its pages will find you knitting a Williamsburg sweater, a Wedgewood sweater, a Paul Gaugin sweater; a sweater with meaning.

Or, better, locate a course in Color Theory based on the work of Josef Albers. Class exercises with silk screened papers, or any colored papers, paint chips for that matter, point out the action and interaction of colors; how they influence and change each other through illusion. Apply these theories to your yarn.

To experiment for possible stripe sequences, select four colors. Cut the paper into strips of the same length, but vary the widths from wide to narrow. Move and switch the stripes until they are in an arrangement that is pleasing to you. Take note of the fact that the same color may speak softly, yell loudly, or completely change face due to its width and the influence exerted on it by its neighbors. Having achieved a persuasive arrangement, paste the strips to a cardboard, and translate the colors and widths to a sample with yarn. The sequence may be repeated throughout the whole sweater, or worked only once in the body, the yoke, or the sleeves.

Play the Odds. Buy the odd dye lot, trade a leftover skein, or splurge on an ounce or two of handspun yarn. Odd unto themselves, not enough for a complete project, but the heart and soul of creativity. Think back to the old patchwork quilt created with what was on hand; the clever quilter turned her scraps into an original, and now treasured, heirloom. So, seek out the odds. Don't pass up a sale or a bargain; a marked down dusty skein of white can be dyed; to go through that process it doesn't have to be pristine. And don't worry about "having enough." Running out could be the best thing that ever happened to you and your sweater.

In the planning stage, take a tip from Nature. Count the petals on a flower; an odd number—which is why "he always loves me" and you're still searching for that four leaf clover. Design your sweater with this concept in mind. Think odd numbers—three colors, five stripes, seven row patterns. If you have only two colors, use one in three places. Your sweater will balance and be pleasing to the eye. Odd numbers hold true for buttons and buttonholes too. The placket neck is best with three and a cardigan with seven or nine.

Rely on Nature. To stand head and shoulders above the crowd, dye your sweater's yarn, all or enough for stripes, with nature's colors. The unusual, unmatchable, and often unpredictable shades may be tossed together or used alone to create your very own impressive effects. To be dyed, the yarn must be in skeins tied in four spots with figure 8's of cotton string. Use a white or an off-white wool yarn for the best results.

---

*Margaret Walch, *The Color Source Book.*

The day before: Gather your dyestuff—a grocery bag full for a pound of yarn (16 ounces), or, a quarter bag full for a four ounce skein. Collect any one of the following: marigolds, zinnias, dahlias, goldenrod, Queen Ann's Lace, dyer's broom, tree bark (apple, oak, birch, or maple), or good old onion skins. If permissible, take the stems and leaves as well as the flower blossoms. Chop as salad, or break in pieces—depending on what you have gathered—and put to soak in an enamel pot with cold water to cover.

The night before: Wash the skeined yarn in order to remove any sizing, starch, or other foreign substances that may have been added during processing. Use a mild soap in lukewarm water, and rinse twice in the same water temperature.

The yarn is now ready for mordanting. This procedure is your assurance that the color will stay fixed to the yarn. A mordant of alum may be used for any of the above listed dyestuffs. Check your local drug store to find if it is available in powder form.

Alum Mordant*

1 lb. dry wool (16 oz.)	¼ lb. dry wool (4 oz.)
4 oz. alum	1 oz. alum
1 oz. cream of tartar	¼ oz. cream of tartar
4 gals. of water	1 gallon of water

Dissolve the alum and the cream of tartar in cold water. Immerse the wet yarn. Gradually heat to boiling; boil gently for one hour, turning and stirring so that all areas of the yarn are exposed to the mordant as equally as possible. Leave the yarn in the mordant overnight.

The morning of: Rinse the mordanted yarn in lukewarm water; let it sit. Bring the dyestuff to a boil for 15 to 30 minutes (bark may take 1 to 2 hours). The boiling time varies; keep checking the liquid for color. Strain the dyestuff from the liquid, and add cold water to replace that which was lost in boiling. Immerse the wet yarn. Gradually bring the pot to boiling for 20 to 30 minutes. Again, keep checking the color by stirring and lifting the yarn with a wooden spoon. The yarn will dry lighter, so let it get a shade darker than what you want. Rinse in lukewarm water until the rinse is clear. Hang the skein to dry.

The dye bath may be reused until the color is gone; the yarns will become lighter in value, and thus blend well together. Other mordants will produce different colors with the same dyestuff; brass, tin, iron, or copper are the most common and may also be purchased in powder form—your ancestors simply changed pots.

*Rita J. Adrosko, *Natural Dyes and Home Dyeing,* p. 68.

A Cardigan (p. 151) with twisted rib neck and cuffs coordinates with handwoven yardage in the same yarn—woven by the author's daughter, Nancy Fee. The warp color sequence is aster, cinnabar, oatmeal, oatmeal; weft sequence is cinnabar, oatmeal, oatmeal, oatmeal.

Right: *A man's Crew Neck (p. 123) has an allover textured "Harris Tweed" stitch. And a Cardigan Jacket (p. 153) of handspun Karakul is worked in Garter Stitch Rib up to the true rib neck shaping.*

Left: *The Placket Neck (p. 137) of the top sweater, along with ribbings, is worked in contrasting wool. The Reversible Sweater (p. 160) shows off the true beauty of seamless construction—inside or out. And a quick and simple camisole is the Basic Sweater worked up to the underarm, then laced and strapped.*

Patterns

Most any pattern stitch may be worked into The Basic Sweater, from a simple double moss stitch to an intricate Aran Isle. In the latter case, you may set-up your own choice of decorative panels, and take them right to the side "seams"; you will have no need for seed stitches with a sewn seam down their middle.

Except for the Aran Isle, and other sweaters with large varying patterns, work the gauge sample in your chosen pattern stitch to see if it is appropriate for your choice of yarn. Beyond that, you will discover whether or not you enjoy working the selected pattern. Some are tedious and not worth the effort. It's best to find this out before embarking on a whole sweater. You may decide to confine the pattern to the yoke, or, use a few inches of it in the body, and/or the sleeves.

To gauge an Aran Isle is almost an impossible task, for each panel will have its own amount of pull-in; even working a hat first will not give you the total effect. The easiest solution seems to be the addition of about 4″ worth of stitches added to the Key Number after working the gauge in plain stockinette stitch. For outerwear, which these sweaters generally are, it is best to be larger than smaller.

Pattern selection hints. Keep the following points in mind when *selecting* an all-over pattern stitch:

1. Select a pattern with a multiple of stitches that closely fits into your Key Number of stitches. Adding, or subtracting one or two stitches is fine, but above that, you may be dealing with an inch or more, added to, or subtracted from the final width of the sweater.

2. To contradict all of the above: if you decide on a large pattern, such as The Dedham Bunny, with its multiple of 22 stitches plus one, or two, for separation, you will have to decide whether you want to go larger or smaller by a good amount of stitches in some cases. Or, rather than have them running around, you could settle for just one in a surprising spot. However, to knit just one of any design, in the round, can be a bit of a nuisance. You certainly don't want to carry the design color around and around to work a few stitches in one spot. The best solution is to work the isolated pattern with separate lengths of yarn; but that procedure leaves the inside full of ends. The other alternative is Swiss Darning.

3. Select a pattern with a plain knit, or plain purl, round if possible. This simplifies the joining round. In bottom-up sweaters, the body and the sleeves *must* stop at the underarm on the same pattern round. Then, when the three pieces are united, all is in order for the yoke. Stopping before a plain knit, or, a plain purl, and using *it* for the joining round, allows you to concentrate on the joining before you return to the pattern.

4. Allover ribbing patterns fit like a second skin. If you prefer a loose fitting sweater, avoid them—unless, like the Reversible Sweater, the rib is accomplished by more knits than purls, or vice versa. Another good choice is the Garter Stitch Rib, p. 14.

5. Select a pattern that is applicable to round and flat knitting, for you must work it both ways in the sweater; round for the body, sleeves, and some of the yoke; flat when the neck shaping is started. Directions for most patterns are written for flat knitting. You may have to reverse the even-numbered rows; an easy job if they are plain knit, or plain purl.

6. Again, because most patterns are written for flat knitting, there may be an extra stitch added beyond the multiple that is not needed in round knitting.

7. In a gem of a booklet, *Double-Knitting Patterns,** Janetta Dexter has compiled a collection of two-color knitting designs, written and graphed, to be worked in the round. Throughout her native Nova Scotia she travelled with pen in hand, and put to paper patterns that previously existed in memory; patterns that had been brought to her country from Great Britain, France, and Germany. These designs, with their quilt-like names, may be worked in commercial yarns, or as they always were, "in homespun wool in natural shades of black, white, and gray, or in yarns dyed in soft colors with natural dyes." Thank you, Janetta.

Candlelit Windows*—a multiple of 8.
>**Round 1**—Dark.
>**Round 2**—* 1D, 1L, 1D, 1L, 1D, 3L *, repeat * to *.
>**Round 3**—* 2D, 1L, 2D, 3L *, repeat * to *.
>**Round 4**—Repeat Round 2.
>**Round 5**—Dark.
>**Round 6**—* 1D, 3L, 1D, 1L, 1D, 1L *, repeat * to *.
>**Round 7**—* 1D, 3L, 2D, 1L, 1D *, repeat * to *.
>**Round 8**—Repeat Round 6.

Pattern knitting hints. Keep these points in mind when *knitting* an allover pattern stitch:

1. The first round, or row, of the body and the sleeves, is vitally important. It sets up the pattern for the whole sweater. Count, and recount, to be absolutely certain you have the correct multiple.

2. To knit a vertical pattern such as cables, ribs, and so forth, the multiple must divide into your Key Number, not only evenly, BUT, the quotient must be an *even* number so that the back and the front have the same number of vertical panels. See the Reversible Sweater for a fuller explanation, p. 160.

---

*Janetta Dexter, *Double Knitting Patterns,* p. 2. This booklet is published by The Nova Scotia Museum, and is available there, or by mail from the Nova Scotia Government Bookstore, P.O. Box 637, Halifax, Nova Scotia, B3J 2T3.

Left: *A Low V-Neck of soft gray wool (p. 147) is trimmed with a ribbed scarf. Soft peach was the choice for a V-Neck with lace cast-off at neck, cuffs and waist (p. 133). Raised stripes enhance the yoke and waist of this Almost Sleeveless (p. 164) Boat Neck Sweater (p. 119).*

Right: *A Chanel-style cardigan in random stripes of natural wool (p. 153), and a reversible Cardigan Vest (p. 174).*

Above: *A Crew Neck with knitted cord cast-off at the neckline (p. 124) was designed from a color study exercise.*
Below: *The Dedham Bunny of pottery fame makes a charming knitted motif for a U-Neck Sweater (p. 125).*

3. In round knitting, start the pattern at the right seamline in the body, and at the seamline in the sleeve. The rounds must start and end correctly.

4. In the Cardigan Sweater, the pattern is worked between the front borders. Be sure that whatever is next to the border on one side is next to the border on the other, so the meeting fronts will match.

5. To repeat, the body and the sleeves must stop for the underarm on the same pattern row.

6. When working a vertical pattern, adjust the number of underarm stitches to another, if it is more logical. See the Reversible Sweater, p. 160.

7. When working a horizontal pattern, you may have to adjust a stitch or two after the joining round. Make any necessary adjustment at the joining points.

8. Most important: the sleeves of a sweater are usually longer than the body. In a sweater with a pattern, or a stripe in sequence, you must take this discrepancy into consideration. Either account for the excess length at the start of the sleeve, or just before the upperarm. The pattern, or the stripe itself, will usually dictate the solution. Generally, it is best to put the excess rounds at the start of the sleeve. Then at the point where the sleeve meets up with the first round of body pattern, repeat the body pattern in the sleeve to the underarm.

Suggested Patterns

Directions are for round knitting. Reverse as you start working back and forth for the neck shaping. These patterns have a plain knit or plain purl round you may use for the joining round.

Hurdle Stitch—a multiple of 2.
Round 1—Knit
Round 2—Purl
Round 3—*K1, P1*, repeat * to *.
Round 4—*K1, P1*, repeat * to *.

Pebble Stitch—a multiple of 2.
Round 1—Knit
Round 2—Knit
Round 3—*K2tog.*, repeat * to *.
Round 4—*P1,P into the horizontal thread before the next stitch.* Repeat * to *.

Waffle Stitch—a multiple of 3
Round 1—*K2, P1*, repeat * to *.
Round 2—*K2, P1*, repeat * to *.
Round 3—*K2, P1*, repeat * to *.
Round 4—Purl

Granite Ridges—a multiple of 2
> **Round 1**—Knit
> **Round 2**—Knit
> **Round 3**—Knit
> **Round 4**—Knit
> **Round 5**—Knit
> **Round 6**—*K2tog.*, repeat * to *.
> **Round 7**—*K1, P1, into each stitch*, repeat * to *
> **Round 8**—Knit.

Harris Tweed Stitch—a multiple of 4
> **Rounds 1 & 2**—Knit.
> **Rounds 3 & 4**—K2, P2.
> **Rounds 5 & 6**—Purl.
> **Rounds 7 & 8**—K2, P2.

Alternating Seed Stitch—a multiple of 2
> **Round 1**—K1, P1.
> **Round 2**—Knit.
> **Round 3**—P1, K1.
> **Round 4**—Knit.

All patterns: *Knitting Dictionary, 1300 Stitches and Patterns.* Pages 42, 75, 77, 79, 84, and 86.

The Turtleneck, **top,** *folds over twice for extra warmth; a purl stripe separates color changes and trims the bottom edge of its Afterthought Pocket. Semi sleeve, Raglan Seamline B. Ringing the Changes is worked in five colors (see p. 103); two Turtles-to-Go offer it a change of looks.*

THE VARIATIONS

The variations presuppose that you have worked the Basic Sweater. Your gauge samples and your numbers on Gauge Page, will vary accordingly with your choice of yarns. *The construction remains constant,* except for the neckline set-ups; check the Decision Points for each style.

The Turtleneck

The turtleneck is one of the easiest and simplest neck variations. The established neck stitches are increased in number for both comfort and looks; there is nothing sadder than a scrawny turtle. The best ribbing pattern is K2, P2, as it retains its shape and elasticity.

Decision Point:
- Work the Basic Sweater, the Crew Neck, through the round establishing the neck ribbing stitches.
- *Stop* after you have worked the back neck stitches from the body needle.
- Put a marker on the right end of the ribbing size needle.

The Set-Up:
- Work a knit round increasing the number of stitches by one-fourth. (Increase into every 4th stitch.)

The Neck Ribbing:
- Count the number of stitches on the needle.
- Adjust, if necessary, to the correct multiple on the first round of ribbing near a seam line.
- Work the first 2″ or 3″ on the ribbing size needle, then switch to a 16″ body size needle.
- Work in ribbing for the desired depth; about 6″ to roll over once; about 9″ to roll over twice.
- Cast off in ribbing loosely.

Or, try a Turtle-To-Go*: Worked separately, this turtle keeps you snug at the bus, but can be doffed easily in the heat of your destination. Work several in colors to match a striped crew; then, like a chameleon, change your accent color to suit the mood of the day.

Turtle-To-Go:
- Count the number of neck ribbing stitches on the matching sweater.
- Increase the number by one-fourth.
- Adjust, if necessary, to the correct multiple for your ribbing pattern.
- Cast the required number of stitches onto a circular 16″ body size needle. Work 3″. Switch to a 16″ ribbing size needle and work 3″. Then return to the 16″ body size needle for the final 3″.
- Bind off in ribbing loosely.

Turtle-To-Go. *Worked with five colors, "Ringing the Changes" provides the sequence, and rhythm, to this Crew Neck sweater. It changes its mood with the addition of a coordinating Turtle-To-Go, a sort of removable "neck warmer".*

*Thank you, Connie Pearlstein.

The Boat Neck

The boat neck does not require any back neck shaping; the front and the back are on an even keel.

Decision Point:

- Work the Basic Sweater, the Crew Neck, to the point where you have 20 stitches remaining to be decreased on each sleeve.
- *Stop* at the right front seam line.

The Set-Up:

- Slip one-half of the stitches onto another circular needle, and try on the sweater.
- Assume the inch's worth of neck ribbing to be added and, if the neck is sitting where you want it, fine. Slip the slipped stitches back onto the body needle and proceed to the Neck Ribbing.
- If not, slip the slipped stitches back onto the body needle, and work a few more decrease rounds, in sequence, then, repeat the try-on. When the neck position is correct, proceed to the Neck Ribbing.

The Neck Ribbing:

- Count the number of stitches on the needle.
- Adjust, if necessary, to the correct multiple on the first round of ribbing near a seamline.
- Using a ribbing size needle, either 16″ or 24″ (the length depends on the size of the sweater, and the number of available stitches), work in ribbing pattern for about an inch.
- Bind off in ribbing loosely.

The Boat Neck. *Knit of a crudely spun off-white yarn, this Almost Sleeveless Sweater stops for a Boat Neck. As there is no back neck shaping, the sweater may be worn fore, or aft. The Raised Stripe, of the same yarn naturally dyed with sandalwood, gives full vent to the teture of the handspun. Seamline A shapes the yoke. Worked on the plain knit rounds, it disappears under the stripes and causes no interference to their continuity.*

The Crew Neck—The Purl Stripe. *A small amount of leftover hand-spun camel hair, found a niche as a purl stripe on a stockinette background of an off-white, commercially spun, lightweight wool yarn; a pleasing mix of wheel and mill. The purl stripes, worked with 7 rounds of stockinette between, are decreased in an orderly fashion throughout the yoke with Seamline B-Reverse.*

The Crew Neck. *From the boy's department—a Crew Neck sweater of oatmeal wool is livened with stripes just before its joining round. The yoke is shaped with Seamline C for a sturdy, rugged look.*

The Crew Neck—Candlelit Windows. *Janetta Dexter is the source for the two-color pattern in the yoke of this Crew Neck sweater knit of a very dark brown handspun wool yarn. The 8-stitch pattern simply plunked itself into a round with its correct multiple, and worked its way to the top, being decreased as it fell with Seamline A for the raglan shaping. The windows are "lit" with handspun; first in a dark steel gray, then in a medium brown, and finally with a light gray mixed and spun with Samoyed dog hair.*

The Crew Neck—Harris Tweed Stitch. *Exactly the same, inside or out, Harris Tweed Stitch is another good choice for a reversible sweater. This simple 8-round pattern produces highlights and shadows that complement the subtle gray shadings of its handspun wool yarn. Seamline A shapes the yoke so as to avoid a prominent seamline interrupting the sequence of the pattern.*

The Crew Neck—Knitted Cord Neckline. *This version of the Crew Neck has its neckline cast off with a Knitted Cord, a change of pace from ribbing. Knit of four colors, the sweater's random stripe sequence was first arranged with strips of silk screen papers in varying widths, then translated into a fabric sample, and finally became the body of the sweater. The sleeves follow the same sequence once their excess length is worked. The two-color work that brightens the yoke is simply achieved by alternating stitches.*

The "Dedham Bunny". *Authentically white within a blue ground, these "Dedham Bunnies" are worked in a reverse color treatment. Here, in indigo blue, they sit in a circle around the body and sleeves of an off-white, lightweight wool sweater. The deep U-Neck is treated to a matching indigo stripe in its ribbing. The ribbing is K2, P2, and the Raglan Seamline Decrease is B.*

The U-Neck

The U-Neck may be started anywhere in the yoke of the sweater. Remember that it will have an inch of ribbing added to it, so start it an inch lower than you want it.

Decision Point:
- Work the Basic Sweater, the Crew Neck, through the joining round.
- *Stop* at the right front seamline anywhere in the straight 1½", or, for a higher U-neck, at the start of a decrease round.

The Set-Up:
- Count the number of stitches on one sleeve. Take this count between the markers in the straight 1½"; between the seamlines if the raglan decreases have started.
- Divide the number of stitches on one sleeve by 2, and add 4. The answer is the number of stitches to leave on the needle at each side front next to the sleeves.
- Run a scrap through the remaining center front stitches.
- Starting at the right front seamline, work to the center front stitches.
- Remove the needle from these stitches.
- *Turn. Stop. Read.* You will now be working back and forth on the needle. If you are working in a pattern, you may have to reverse your knits and purls on the inside rows, *and,* before this next inside row you may have to work a catch-up row over the stitches from the right neck edge *to* the decrease at the right front seamline. If you have started the raglan decreases, or when you do:

    The *outside rows* are the decrease rows.
    The *inside rows* are the straight rows.

    From now on, start all rows with a slip stitch for a chain selvedge:
    Outside rows—Slip as if to purl, yarn in back.
    Inside rows—Slip as if to purl, yarn in front.
- *Work the inside row.*
- *On the next 4 outside rows only,* decrease 1 stitch at the neck edges, and continue to decrease at the raglan seamlines:

    Start and end these next 4 outside rows:
    Slip 1, K2tog., work to the last 3 stitches, SSK, K1.
- *Then,* continue the decreases at the raglan seamlines until the seamlines come together and the sleeve is gone.
- *Stop* at the end of an outside row.

The Neck Ribbing:
- Using a 24" circular ribbing size needle, knit into the left side neck chain selvedge, knit the stitches from the scrap (slip them onto a double-point), knit into the right side neck chain selvedge, and knit the back neck stitches from the body needle.
- Count the number of stitches on the needle. If the number must be adjusted for the ribbing pattern, do so in the first round of ribbing near a raglan seamline.

- Put a marker on the right needle and work the ribbing pattern loosely for an inch.
- Cast off in ribbing loosely.

The U-Neck. *The U-Neck is a most comfortable sweater. It affords more room than the Crew when worn over a coordinating blouse or turtleneck jersey; and of course, it shows off more of that coordinating effort. This particular version is knit of two colors that follow Fibonacci's sequence from below the joining round up, a move that necessitates knowing the approximate number of rows in the yoke. The colors alternate using the sequence double, and in reverse, from 13, 13; 8, 8; 5, 5; 3, 3; 2, 2; 1, 1. In fact, a few extra 1, 1's were needed to reach the top. The yoke shaping is accomplished with Seamline E, perhaps not the best choice as its "feathers" somewhat vie for attention with the featured stripe sequence.*

The V-Neck

Decision Point:

- Work the Basic Sweater, the Crew Neck, through the joining round.
- Work a few rounds of the straight 1½ ".
- **Stop** at the right front seamline **6** rounds before the first raglan seamline decrease.

The Set-Up:

- Count the number of front stitches between the markers. You must have an uneven number. K2tog. before the marker at the right front seamline if you must adjust.
- Put a safety pin *through* the center front stitch. Check to be sure that you have an equal number of stitches on each side of the pin.
- Starting at the right front seamline, work around to the stitch on the pin.
- Remove the left needle from this stitch. Be sure it is secure on the pin.
- **Turn. Stop. Read. Find a pencil.**

The Math:

You must figure how many times to work a decrease at the neck edges for the V-shaping. If you decrease too many times, you will run out of front stitches before the sleeve is gone. If you decrease too few times, you will have front stitches remaining after the sleeve is gone. The sleeve stitches and the front stitches must disappear at the same time.

As you decrease at the right and left front raglan seamlines, you are eating up one stitch from each side front with one stitch from each sleeve; equally they go, hand in hand. By finding how many stitches are excess to each side front, above and beyond the number needed to decrease each sleeve, you will know how many times to work a decrease at each neck edge.

As the number of times to decrease will be the same for the right and left neck shaping, concentrate on the right half front for the figuring:

- Count the number of stitches in the right half of the front.
- Count the number of stitches on the right sleeve. As only half the sleeve stitches are decreased at the front raglan seamline (the other half are decreased at the back raglan seamline), divide the number of stitches on the right sleeve by 2.
- Subtract the one-half sleeve from the right half of the front.
- The answer is the number of stitches that are excess to the right half front and are not needed to decrease the right sleeve. Therefore, that is the number of times to work a decrease at the right neck edge, *and* the left neck edge.
- Keep this number in the back of your head for the moment, or, jot it down here _____.

Your math is done. Return to the sweater.

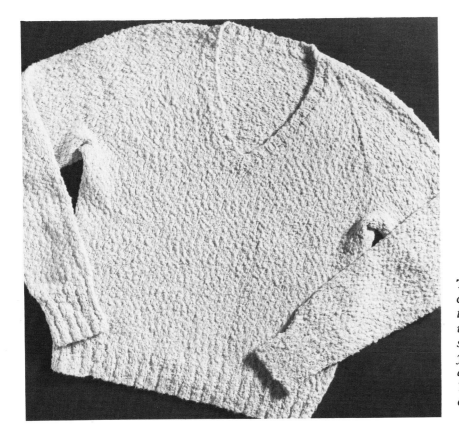

The V-Neck. *An off-white cotton flake yarn provides all the texture of this V-Neck worked in plain stockinette stitch. Seamline A shapes the yoke and practically disappears into the rough surface. The sweater may be worn either side out.*

A "champagne" fleece with two distinct shadings was so divided, carded, and spun into yarns of light and dark. The lighter, thickly spun, was just enough for a warm V-Neck laced with a Knitted Cord. Plain stockinette stitch was all that was needed to promote the "puffed wheat" texture of the yarn. Seamline A shapes the yoke.

The Neck Shaping:

You will now be working back and forth on the needle. If you are working in a pattern, you may have to reverse your knits and purls on the inside rows, *and,* before this next inside row, you may have to work a catch-up row over the stitches from the right neck edge *to* the right front seamline.

- Work the inside row to the end of the needle. From now on, start all rows with a slip stitch for a chain selvedge:
  Outside rows—slip as if to purl, yarn in back.
  Inside rows—slip as if to purl, yarn in front.
- On the next outside row, and every *other* outside row thereafter for as many times as are necessary, work a decrease at the neck edges:
  Start and end the neck edge decrease rows:
  Slip 1, K2tog., work to the last 3 stitches, SSK, K1.
- Work 3 straight rows.
- On the next outside row, work a decrease at the neck edges, *and,* start the raglan seamline decreases. (As the raglan seamline decreases are worked every 4th row for a while, and the neck edge decreases are worked every 4th row, combining them in the next row starts you off in orderly fashion, and gives you 3 straight rows to follow. Once the raglan seamline decreases start their every other row sequence, this respite of 3 straight rows will end.)

So, working the raglan seamline decreases in their proper order, and the neck edge decreases every fourth row, head for the top. When you are nearly there, stop for a quick number check:

- Count the stitches remaining to be decreased on the right sleeve. Do not count between the markers and do not include the seamline stitches in this count. Divide by 2.
- Count the number of stitches on the right side front. Again, do not count from the marker and do not include the seamline in this count. If you have finished your neck edge decreases, these numbers should be equal, and all is well. If the numbers are not equal, and the front has more stitches than half the sleeve, the difference is the number of times to continue decreasing at the neck edge.

If for any reason half the sleeve is more than the front, you're in trouble. If the difference is only a stitch or two, K3tog. at the next sleeve decrease, or work a decrease on a straight row. Check the situation at the left side front and left sleeve as well.

When the seamlines come together, and the fronts and sleeves are gone, ***stop*** at the end of an outside row.

The Neck Ribbing:

Using a 16″ or 24″ circular needle (the length depends on the size of the sweater, and the number of available stitches), *one* size smaller than the body:

- Knit into the left side neck chain selvedge,
- Knit the stitch from the pin,
- ***Put a marker on the needle,***
- Knit into the right side neck chain selvedge, and,
- Knit the back neck stitches from the body needle. ***Stop.***

To hold the V-neck flat and open to its proper depth, it is necessary to increase a few stitches in the middle of each side. It is also necessary to work the center stitch of the V, the stitch before the marker, as a **knit** throughout the ribbing, *and* this center knit stitch must start out with a purl, or purls, beside it.

Being conscious of all of the above, proceed cautiously to the first round of your ribbing pattern.

- As you work the ribbing down the left side, visually keep back-tracking from the center knit stitch, picturing the purl, or purls, beside it, and plan your few increases accordingly.
- Work the bar increase into a knit stitch that will be followed by a purl on the next round; assume the bump of the bar increase to be that purl.
- *Knit* the stitch before the marker.
- As you start up the right side, work a purl, or purls, after the center knit stitch, and increase the same number of stitches on this side as you did on the other.
- Now, look ahead to be certain that your ribbing pattern will end correctly as you finish the first round. Adjust near a seamline if necessary.
- On the next round, and every *other* round thereafter, decrease 1 stitch on each side of the center knit stitch to miter the point of the V. Use your discretion as whether to K2tog., or P2tog., depending on your ribbing pattern.
- Work the ribbing pattern loosely for about an inch.
- Bind off in ribbing loosely.

Variation—The Lace Edging:

- Work the V-Neck through the round establishing the neck stitches. Upon completion of this round, the needles are positioned at the left shoulder. To start the lace cast-off, they must be at the base of the V, so,
- Slip all the stitches for the left side of the neck onto the right needle, including the center stitch.
- Remove the marker. The needles are now at the base of the V. The yarn is still at the left shoulder. Break it and secure it there.
- Tie (for security) the yarn into the first stitch on the left needle at the base of the V.
- Count the number of stitches on the needle.

To work the sampler lace, you must have a multiple of 4 stitches. Or, if you select a different lace, you must have its multiple. Keep in mind the number of stitches you must adjust, if any, and do so while working the lace near a back seamline.

- With the outside facing, and with a double-pointed ribbing size needle in your right hand, insert the tip of the needle in between the first two stitches on the left needle, and proceed to:
- Cast 5 stitches onto the left needle.
- Knit the 5 stitches.
- Turn your work.
- Your are now in a position to work the lace edging as in the sampler, p. 43, starting with Row 1.

To refresh your memory: it is only at the end of rows 2, 4, 6, and 8, that you are casting off 1 stitch of the neck by knitting a stitch of the lace together with a stitch of the neck. It therefore takes 2 rows of lace work to cast off 1 stitch. In the sampler the lace stitches were of a different color and easily discernible. In the sweater they may be one and the same. Work the lace rows carefully and be sure each row ends on the correct stitch.

- Work the cast-off up the right side neck, across the back neck, and down the left side neck, ending where you started at the base of the V.
- On the last row of lace, when you are to cast off the last neck stitch, bind off all the lace stitches, not just the first four. At the base of the V the lace edges overlap, and may be left loose, or sewed together.

To add matching lace at the sleeve cuff:

If you planned ahead and worked the invisible cast-on, remove the auxiliary yarn, and put the stitches on three double-points.

- Starting at the seamline, tie in new yarn, and cast 5 stitches onto the needle. Proceed as above.
- If you did not plan ahead, snip one-half stitch in the row above the ribbing. Carefully unravel horizontally and drop the ribbing off. Put the exposed stitches on three double-points and proceed as above.

The V-Neck—Lace Edged. *Here, the V-Neck is cast off with lace in the same pattern as that of the sweater sampler, an ample width for a delicate trim to a soft peach sweater. For the sleeve cuffs and the body, the lace was added after the fact; and the body lace is further "laced" with the Knitted Cord.*

The Slit Neck. *The Gauge Sample set the direction for this sweater. Its purl side proved a better foil for the "neppy" light gray handspun yarn, and so the sweater progressed with its purl side outside; a matter of no real consequence, as the sweater is reversible. The yoke shaping was accomplished working Seamline B on the inside rows; thus the seamline you see here is the inside of Seamline B. To have worked the sweater on the knit side and worn it inside out would perhaps have made more sense, but it made for more pleasant knitting looking at the sweater's better side. Its slit is laced with a Twisted Cord of matching yarn. The Mushroom Cap is a random stripe of gray and white handspun topped with a Knitted Loop.*

The Slit Neck

Decision Point:

- Work the Basic Sweater, the Crew Neck, to within 2 rounds of the start of the raglan seamline decreases.
- *Stop* at the right front seamline. (If you want a shorter slit, stop at the right front seamline at the start of any decrease round.)

The Set-Up:

Note: The directions assume a 6 stitch Cardigan Border on each side of the slit. If you want a wider border, substitute 8 or 10 for the 6's.

- Count the number of front stitches. You must have an even number. K2tog. before the marker at the right front seamline if you must adjust.
- Tie a yarn marker around the needle at the center of the front.
- Check to be sure there is an equal number of stitches in each half of the front sections.
- Starting at the right front seamline, work to the yarn marker.
- *Turn.* You now have the inside of the sweater facing.
- *Stop. Read.*

You will now be working back and forth on the needle. If you are working in a pattern, you may have to reverse your knits and purls on the inside rows, *and,* before the next inside row, you may have to work a catch-up row over the stitches from the right neck edge *to* the right front seamline.

- Work the inside row.
- *Turn.*
- On the next outside row, work the first 6 stitches and the last 6 stitches in Cardigan Border, *and,* start the raglan seamline decreases. Refer to Cardigan Border, page 17.
- Continue to work back and forth on the needle keeping the first and last 6 stitches in Cardigan Border on both the outside and the inside rows, *and,* work the raglan seamline decreases in their proper order.
- *And,* if you want to lace the slit, work a buttonhole at each end of the needle using the substitute beginning *and* ending of Row 1 at appropriate intervals.
- Work until 20 or 21 stitches remain to be decreased on each sleeve.
- *Stop* at the beginning of an outside row.

The Neck Shaping and the Neck Ribbing:

Refer to the Placket Neck.

The Placket Neck

Decision Point:
- Work the Basic Sweater, the Crew Neck, to within 2 rounds of the start of the raglan seamline decreases.
- *Stop* at the right front seamline.

The Set-Up:
   Note: This set-up is for a placket neck in a woman's sweater. For a man's, see Placket Neck Variation on page 139. The directions assume a 6 stitch Cardigan Border for each side of the placket opening. For 8 or 10 stitch borders, see the variation on page 139.
- Count the number of front stitches between the markers. You must have an even number. K2tog. before the marker at the right front seamline if you must adjust.
- Tie a yarn marker around the needle at the center of the front. Check to be sure there is an equal number of stitches in each half of the front sections.
- Starting at the right front seamline, work to within 3 stitches of the center front marker.
- *Turn.* You now have the inside of the sweater facing you.
- Insert the right needle in between the first two stitches on the left needle and proceed to:
- Cast 6 stitches onto the left needle.
- *Stop. Read.*
   You will now be working back and forth on the needle. If you are working in a pattern, you may have to reverse your knits and purls on the inside rows, *and,* before this next inside row, you might have to work a catch-up row over the unworked front stitches from the right neck edge to the right front seamline.
- Purl the 6 cast-on stitches, and work the inside row to the end. The end is the point where the opening has been made—3 stitches beyond the yarn marker. This marker may now be removed.
- *Turn.*
- On the next outside row, work the first 6 stitches and the last 6 stitches (the cast-ons), in Cardigan Border, *and,* start the raglan seamline decreases. Refer to Cardigan Border.
   When completed, the 6 cast-on stitches are tacked down inside the sweater. This is the button side of the placket. The 6 stitches at the beginning of the outside rows form the buttonhole side of the placket.
- Work the first buttonhole about 1″ above the opening; the second about 2″ above the first; and the third in the neck ribbing. (The placement of the second buttonhole is a bit tricky. The third one in the neck ribbing is made in a position roughly corresponding to the point at which the neck shaping begins, i.e., when 20 stitches remain to be decreased on each sleeve. Be sure to put the second buttonhole in well before this point.)

• Continue to work back and forth on the needle, keeping the first and last 6 stitches in Cardigan Border on both the outside and the inside rows, and work the raglan seam line decreases in their proper order.

The Placket Neck. *This brown handspun wool, placket neck sweater has its ribbings and neckline worked with leftover handspun in dark "champagne". Counting the two sleeve ribbings as one, the sweater is a successful example of "playing the odds"; if you have only two colors, use one in three places. The buttons are quiet.*

- Work until 20 or 21 stitches remain to be decreased on each sleeve.
- **Stop** at the beginning of an outside row.

The Neck Shaping:
- Work the outside row *to* within 15 stitches of the *seamline.*
- Slip the stitches you have just worked onto a holder.
- Continue working across the row *to* the 15th stitch after the last *seamline* decrease.
- Slip the remaining stitches onto a holder. (If it bothers you, or your pattern, that these stitches you are slipping on the holder will be minus one row of work in the final accounting, work to the end of the row and break the yarn. To work to the end of the row and head back, they would have one more in the final accounting. Tie the yarn in 14 stitches from the *seamline.* Slip the stitches that are on the needle before the yarn onto a holder.)
- Check to be sure that the stitches on the holders are equal in number.
- Check to be sure that there are 14 stitches at each end of the needle before the front raglan seamlines.
- **Turn,** and work the inside row. You will now be working back and forth on the stitches between the holders. Start all rows with a slip stitch for a chain selvedge:
    Outside rows—slip as if to purl, yarn in back.
    Inside rows—slip as if to purl, yarn in front.
- **On the next 4 outside rows only,** decrease 1 stitch at the neck edges, and continue to decrease at the raglan seam lines: start and end these next 4 outside rows:
    Slip 1, K2tog., work to the last 3 stitches, SSK, K1.
- **Then,** continue the decreases at the raglan seamlines until the seamlines come together and the sleeve is gone.
- **Stop** at the end of an inside row. Break the yarn, and secure.

The Neck Ribbing:
    Slip the stitches from the holders to double-points to work them. With the outside facing you, connect the yarn at the beginning of the outside row, and using a 24″ circular ribbing size needle in your right hand:
- Work the stitches from the holder, keeping the first 6 in Cardigan Border (**Decision Point:** Hood. Put a marker on the needle)
- Knit into the right side neck chain selvedge,
- Knit the back neck stitches from the body needle,
- Knit into the left side neck chain selvedge (**Hood**. Put a marker on the needle)
- Work the stitches from the last holder, keeping the last 6 in Cardigan Border.
- **Stop.**
- Count the number of stitches in *between* the borders.
    You are going to start the neck ribbing pattern on the next

row—an inside row—but do your thinking and planning looking at the outside. As Cardigan Border continues on the first and last 6 stitches throughout the ribbing, it must have a knit, or knits, beside it. Therefore:

> For K1, P1 ribbing, you must have an uneven number of stitches.
>
> For K2, P2 ribbing, you must have a number of stitches divisible by 4, plus 2.

Keeping in mind the number of stitches to adjust, if necessary, near a seamline and, ***thinking in reverse,***

- Work the inside row of neck ribbing.
- ***Turn.*** Before continuing, check the line-up of the knits and purls.
- Work the neck ribbing loosely for about an inch, adding one more buttonhole.
- Stop at the end of an inside row.
- Bind off loosely in ribbing.
- Tack the buttonhole side of the placket to the inside.

Placket Neck Variations

For a Placket in a Man's Sweater:
- Follow the preceding directions through the set-up.
- ***Then,*** to reverse the opening: starting at the right front seamline, work 3 stitches *beyond* the center front marker.
- ***Turn,*** and work the inside row to the end.
- ***Turn,*** and cast 6 stitches onto the left needle.
- Work the 6 cast-on stitches in Cardigan Border; work across the row to within the last 6 stitches; work these last 6 stitches in Cardigan Border.

    The 6 cast-on stitches are the button side of the placket. The 6 stitches at the end of the outside row form the buttonhole side of the placket.
- Refer back to the preceding directions to complete the sweater.

For a Shorter Placket Opening:
- ***Stop*** at the right front seamline after a straight round. The set-up is the same as for the preceding directions, except you must count the number of stitches **between the seamlines,** not between the markers. The working of the sweater is the same except you have already started your raglan seamline decreases.
- Refer back to the preceding directions to complete the sweater.

For Wider Cardigan Borders:
The set-up is the same as for the 6 stitch border *except:* for an 8 stitch border, work to within 4 stitches of the center front marker, etc., and then, cast 8 stitches onto the left needle.

For a 10 stitch border, work to within 5 stitches of the center front marker, etc., and then, cast 10 stitches onto the left needle.

The remaining directions are the same, except substitute your 8 or 10 for the 6's.

For a placket in a contrasting color:

- Wind two small balls of yarn.
- Work the preceding directions to the point where the 6 stitches are to be cast onto the left needle.
- Connect one ball of yarn to the first stitch on the left needle, and using the contrasting yarn, cast 6 stitches onto the left needle.
- With the contrasting yarn, purl the 6 cast-on stitches.
- With the original yarn, work the inside row to within 6 stitches of the end of the needle.
- Connect the other ball of yarn, and work the last 6 stitches in the contrasting yarn.
- On both the inside and outside rows, work the first and last 6 stitches on the needle in Cardigan Border in the contrasting yarn. Remember to bring the new color from under the old when switching from one to the other to avoid holes.

For an attached hood without a drawstring—loose:

Follow the placket neck directions for the neck ribbing *except* put a marker on the needle *after* the stitches are worked from the first holder, and *before* the stitches are worked from the last holder. Carry these markers throughout the neck ribbing.

- Work the ribbing for about an inch.
- ***Stop*** at the end of an inside row.
- On the next outside row, bind off the stitches before the first marker; increase into every stitch across to the second marker; work straight to the end of the row.
- ***Turn.***
- On the next inside row, bind off the stitches before the first marker, and purl to the end of the row.
- ***Turn.***
- ***Change to a body size 24″*** needle and on both the outside and the inside rows, work the first and last 6 stitches in Cardigan Border.
- *Work back and forth on the needle until the hood is about 5″ above the ribbing, or halfway to the top of your head. On the next outside row, put a marker on the needle before the center stitch.
- On the next outside row, and ***every other outside*** row, work decrease B at this marker to refine the point of the hood.
- Work to the top of the hood, usually 10″ above the ribbing. Or, try on the sweater, and stop working when the sides of the hood meet at the top of your head—comfortably.
- Work the next outside row to the marker.
- ***Stop.*** Break the yarn, leaving a very good yard.
- Thread the end through the Braidkin.
- Slip the remaining unworked stitches onto another needle.

The Hood—Back View. *The Hood develops from the ribbing of the Placket Neck sweater, and by increasing into every stitch of the ribbing, it emerges with soft, comfortable fullness. Halfway to the top, Decrease Seamline B is worked every fourth row to refine its point. Seamline B also shapes the raglan seamlines in the yoke.*

The Placket Neck. *Given the good old gray sweatshirt treatment, this Placket Neck sweater, knit of a medium weight gray wool, is hooded and pocketed; the former grows out of the neck ribbing, and the latter, out of the body ribbing. Thus, as involved as it looks, the sweater is still worked in seamless progression.*

The top of the hood is to be grafted together to produce an invisible seam: hold the needle with the unworked stitches nearest to you—the Front Needle. Hold the needle with the worked stitches farthest from you—the Back Needle. The yarn is coming from the first stitch on the Back Needle, so you are all set to begin grafting. Refer to Grafting in the sampler, p. 54. Treat the last 6 stitches on each needle, those in Cardigan Border, as 3; in other words, graft the 6 stitches two at a time, scooping a purl with a knit. True, this double-dip grafting will not look perfect, but it will be hidden from view once the border rolls to the inside.

For an attached hood with drawstring:

Follow the placket neck directions for the neck ribbing *except,* put a marker on the needle *after* the stitches are worked from the first holder, and *before* the stitches are worked from the last holder. Carry these markers throughout the neck ribbing.

• Work the ribbing for about an inch.
• *Stop* at the end of an inside row.
• On the next outside row, bind off the stitches before the marker, increase into every stitch across to the second marker; work straight to the end of the row.
• *Turn.*
• With the inside facing you, bind off the stitches before the first marker, and purl to the end of the row.
• *Turn.*
• Cast 6 stitches onto the left needle.
• Work the 6 cast-on stitches in Cardigan Border, and work to the end of the row.
• *Turn.*
• Cast 6 stitches onto the left needle.
• Work the 6 cast-on stitches in Cardigan Border; work across the row to within 6 stitches of the end; work the last 6 stitches in Cardigan Border.
• *Turn.*
• Change to a 24″ body size needle and, on both the inside and the outside rows, work the first and last 6 stitches in Cardigan Border, *and* work a buttonhole in the Cardigan Border at each end of the needle one inch above the ribbing:

    Refer to Buttonholes, p. 18. On an outside row substitute the buttonhole beginning and ending of Row 1 for the Normal Cardigan Border.

• Proceed as for the loose hood starting * and working through the grafting.
• Fold the border stitches to the inside and tack down lightly around the edge of the hood to form a casing.
• Run a drawstring through the casing, and tie under the chin.

The Open Raglan

Decision Point:

- Work the Basic Sweater, the Crew Neck, to the first raglan seamline decrease round. To prepare for the upcoming opening, plan to work Decrease C at the left front seamline. As this is a wide seamline, you might want to work another style at the other three.
- Work the yoke to the fourth raglan seamline decrease round.
- *Stop* at the right front seamline.

The Set-Up:

- Work a normal decrease round *through* the first half of the decrease at the left front seamline.
- *Stop. Read.* You will now be working back and forth on the needle.

If you are working in a pattern, you may have to reverse your knits and purls on the inside rows, *and,* as the front of this sweater will be minus one row of work, and also minus the second half of the decrease at the left front seamline (because you couldn't get there), you *must* work a catch-up:

- With a separate length of yarn, and with the outside facing, work the unworked front:
- Starting with the left half of the left front seamline, slip 1, SSK (the missing decrease), work across to the right seamline. Now, back to the body yarn at the left front seamline.
- With the inside facing, work the inside row to the end. The end is the center of the left front seamline.
- *Turn. Stop. Read.*

As you work back and forth on the needle, the rows will start and end in the center of the decrease at the left front seamline. Work the raglan seamline decreases in proper order. Starting and ending the decrease rows:

> *Outside rows:* Slip 1 (as if to purl, yarn in back), SSK, work to within 3 stitches of the end, K2tog., K1.
> *Inside rows:* Slip 1 (as if to purl, yarn in front), work to the end.

The Neck Shaping:

- Work until 20 or 21 stitches remain to be decreased on each sleeve.
- *Stop* at the beginning of an outside row.
- Run a scrap through all the front stitches *except for 14 on each side next to the sleeves.*
- *Read.*

The left side neck shaping is worked separately, and last. The body yarn is attached in a position to work this small triangle of stitches. Do not break it. If you must use the same ball to work the right side neck shaping first, wind off a small amount and leave it attached here.

- Slip all the stitches for the left side neck onto a holder.
- Remove the needle from the center front stitches.
- With a new ball of yarn, and starting with the 14th stitch before the right front seamline, work a decrease row to the center of the left front seamline.
- ***Turn.***
- Work an inside row. You will now be working back and forth on the needle from the right neck edge to the center of the left front seamline.
- Start the ***next 4 outside rows only:***
    Slip 1, K2tog., work to the end.
- ***Then,*** continue the decreases at the raglan seamlines until the seamlines come together and the sleeves are gone.
- ***Stop*** at the end of an outside row.
- Slip the stitches at the left side neck from the holder onto a body size double-point.
- Using body size double-points and the reserved yarn, and with the outside facing, work an outside row over these stitches:
    Slip 1, SSK, work to the end.
- ***Turn.*** Work an inside row. ***Stop. Read.***
    You will now be working back and forth over the left side neck stitches. To duplicate the right side neck shaping, you must decrease at the *end* of the outside rows, (as well as continuing the raglan decrease at the beginning):
- ***End*** the next 4 outside rows only:
    Work to within 3 stitches of the end, SSK, K1.
- Then continue the decrease at the left front seamline until this triangle of stitches matches the shaping of the right neck edge.
- Stop at the beginning of an outside row—all 2 stitches of it.

The Neck Ribbing:
    Using a ribbing size 24″ circular needle in your right hand,
- Knit the seamline stitches from the double-point,
- Knit into the left side neck chain selvedge,
- Knit the stitches from the scrap (slip them onto a double-point),
- Knit into the right side neck chain selvedge,
- Knit the back neck stitches from the body needle.
    Finally, you are all back together again. Count the number of stitches on the needle. As the open edges of the ribbing must match:
    For K1, P1, you must have an uneven number.
    For K2, P2, you must have a number divisible by 4, plus 2. Keeping in mind the number of stitches to adjust, if necessary, in the first row of ribbing near a seamline, *and, thinking **in reverse** for this inside row, *and* substituting a slip 1 for the first stitch of your ribbing pattern:
- Start the ribbing. The inside row:
    Slip 1 (as if to purl, yarn in front, this slip subs for a purl—your next stitch is a knit for K1, P1, or another purl for K2, P2), work to the end of the row, ending either P1 or P2.
- ***Turn.***

- The outside row:

  Slip 1 (as if to purl, yarn in back, this slip subs for a knit— your next stitch is a purl for K1, P1, or another knit for K2, P2).
- Work to the end of the row, ending either K1, or K2.
- Work the neck ribbing loosely for about an inch.
- Bind off in ribbing loosely.
- Crochet button loops on the front edge of the opening.
- Sew the buttons on the back edge of the opening.

The Open Raglan. *With its left front raglan seamline opening, the Crew Neck takes on an asymmetrical air. Trimmed with functional buttons and loops, the opening makes for easier ons and offs—a feature that is much appreciated by occupants of all ages, from babes on up. Seamline C is a must for the left front raglan; the others may be of your choice. The ribbings are K3, P3, for maximum elasticity. Alternating seed stitch adds further interest to the off-white variegated yarn shot with black and rust. The Beaded Rib Scarf coordinates with its seed stitch ribbing pattern.*

The Low V-Neck

Decision Point:

- Work the body of the Basic Sweater, the Crew Neck, to a depth of about 7″, including the ribbing.
- *Stop* at the right seamline.
- Put a marker at the left *seamline*.

The Set-Up:

Note: The directions assume a 6 stitch Cardigan Border on each side of the V-neck. For wider borders, refer to the variations of the Placket Neck, page 137.

- Count the number of front stitches between the markers. You must have an even number. K2tog. before the right seam marker if you must adjust.
- Tie a yarn marker around the needle at the center of the front. Check to be sure there is an equal number of stitches in each half of the front section.
- Starting at the right seamline, work to within 3 stitches of the center front marker.
- *Turn.* You now have the inside of the sweater facing you.
- Insert the right needle in between the first two stitches on the left needle and proceed to:
- Cast 6 stitches onto the left needle.
- *Stop. Read.*

You will now be working back and forth on the needle. If you are working in a pattern, you may have to reverse your knits and purls on the inside rows, *and,* before the next inside row you may have to work a catch-up row over the unworked front stitches to the marker at the right front seamline.

- Purl the 6 cast-on stitches, and work the inside row to the end. The end is the point where the opening has been made—3 stitches beyond the yarn marker.
- *Turn.*
- On this next outside row, work the first 6 stitches and the last 6 stitches (the cast-ons) in Cardigan Border. Refer to Cardigan Border, page 17.

When completed, the 6 cast-on stitches are tacked down inside the sweater. This is the button side of the placket. The 6 stitches at the beginning of the outside rows form the buttonhole side of the placket.

- Work straight for 3″, keeping the first and last 6 stitches in Cardigan Border on both the inside and the outside rows, *and,* work a buttonhole about an inch above the opening; and another about 2″ above the first. Refer to Buttonholes, page 18.
- *Stop* at the beginning of an outside row. *Read.*

The two buttonholes you have worked in the straight placket are the only two that truly button. From now on, work a decrease at the neck edges every 8th row in a fine yarn, every 6th row in a

The Low V-Neck. *Started in the round, the Low V-Neck opens to button twice before veering off below the joining round. K3, P3 ribs the body and the sleeves, and works the on or off scarf which is lavishly fringed with long soft strands of its oxford gray brushed wool. The buttons are pearl; a quick switch to pigskin would change its look. The Seamline is D.*

medium yarn. These decreases at the neck edges start the V shaping. If you intend to decorate the sweater with buttons to the top, you might continue the buttonholes—for effect only—working one about every 2″. If the sweater is to be sans buttons, discontinue the buttonholes.

- On the next outside row, and on every neck edge decrease row thereafter:
   Work the first 6 stitches in Cardigan Border, *K2tog.*, work across to within 8 stitches of the end, *SSK,* work the last 6 stitches in Cardigan Border.
- Continue to work back and forth on the needle, keeping the first and the last 6 stitches in Cardigan Border, *and,* work a decrease at the neck edges every 6th or 8th row.
- Work the body to the underarm.
- ***Stop*** at the beginning of an outside row.

The Sleeves:
- Refer to the Basic Sweater.
- Work the sleeves to the underarm.

Joining—Sleeve Preparation:
Refer to the Basic Sweater.

Joining—Body Preparation:
   The *left* and the *right* underarm: the seamline is the center of the underarm stitches; one-half are to the right, one-half are to the left. Run a scrap yarn through the underarm stitches at each side of the body. Tie loosely. The underarm stitches at each side of the body remain on both the scrap and the needle for the moment.

The Joining Row:
- Work the outside row to the right underarm stitches.
- Remove the left needle from the underarm stitches.
- Refer to the Joining Round of the Basic Sweater and attach the sleeves to the body.
- Work to the end of the outside row.
- Work the inside row. ***Stop. Read.***

   You must figure how many times to work the neck edge decreases. Count the number of stitches in the right front of the sweater. Do not include the 6 stitches of the Cardigan Border in this count. Count the number of stitches on the right sleeve. Divide by 2. Subtract the one-half sleeve from the right front. The difference is the number of times to decrease at each neck edge. Once the excess number of front stitches are decreased at the neck edge, discontinue the neck edge decreases. The remaining front stitches are decreased at the raglan seamlines. Keep a careful count of the number of times (or stitches) that you decrease at the neck edge. If you decrease too many, you will run out of front stitches before the sleeve is gone. If you decrease too few, you will have front stitches remaining after the sleeve is gone. The sleeve stitches and the front stitches must disappear at the same time.

- Continue working back and forth on the needle, keeping the first and last 6 stitches in Cardigan Border, **and** now work a decrease at the neck edges every 6th row in a fine yarn, or every 4th row in a medium yarn, **and** start the raglan seamline decreases. As you near the top, check to be sure your math for the V-Neck shaping is on target.
- **Stop** at the beginning of an outside row when the seamlines come together and the fronts and the sleeves are gone.
- Work the first 6 stitches in Cardigan Border, then slip them onto a holder.
- Bind off all the neck stitches, loosely, to within the last 6 stitches.
- With double-points, work back and forth over the last 6 stitches of Cardigan Border until the strip is long enough to reach the center of the back of the neck.
- Slip the other 6 stitches of Cardigan Border from the holder, and with double-points work the strip until it is long enough to reach the center of the back of the neck.
- Sew the border strips to the bound-off neck edge, and sew or graft the 6 border stitches to each other at the center of the back of the neck. If you opt to graft, treat the 6 stitches as 3; in other words, graft the 6 stitches two at a time, scooping a purl with a knit. True, this double-dip grafting will not be perfect, but to graft the 6 singly will spread them to full width. Grafting them two at a time preserves the ribbing with its hidden purls.

The Cardigan Sweater

- Work a gauge sample.
- Determine the Key Number of stitches.

The Body Ribbing:

This requires a bit more math than usual—follow closely:subtract 10% from the Key Number to determine the number of ribbing stitches. Now, adjust the number of ribbing stitches accordingly for your selected ribbing pattern:

K1, P1, requires an uneven number of stitches.

K2, P2, requires a number of stitches divisible by 4, plus 2.

The adjusted number of ribbing stitches equals _____.

Add 12 stitches to this number for Cardigan Border _____.

This final figure is the number of stitches to cast on to a 24″ circular ribbing size needle. The directions assume a 6 stitch Cardigan Border on each side front. For 8 stitch borders, add 16 stitches. For 10 stitch borders, add 20 stitches. The remaining directions are the same, *except* substitute your 8 or 10 for the 6's, and add an appropriate number of additional K1, P1's, to the first row. ***Stop. Read.***

The First Row:

The body of the cardigan sweater is worked back and forth in the flat on the circular needle. In order that the body cast-on present the same face as the sleeve cast-on, a preliminary *inside* row must be worked. Therefore, the 6 stitches of Cardigan Border at each end of the needle are worked as Row 2.

- Work the following first row according to your chosen ribbing style:

    For K1, P1—P1, K1, P1, K1, P1, K1, then, P1, K1, across to the last 7 stitches, end, *P1,* K1, P1, K1, P1, K1, P1.

    For K2, P2—P1, K1, P1, K1, P1, K1, then, P2, K2, across to the last 8 stitches, end, *P2,* K1, P1, K1, P1, K1, P1.

- ***Turn*** your work. The outside of the sweater is now facing you. Notice that the six stitches of Cardigan Border are now balanced with a knit, or knits, beside them—the result of figuring on an uneven number of stitches for a K1, P1, ribbing, or, figuring a number of stitches divisible by 4, plus 2, for a K2, P2, ribbing. Without this extra stitch, or two, the purl of the border would be next to a purl of the ribbing.

- Now, refer to Cardigan Border, and start with Row 1—the Outside. Throughout the ribbing, you will be working the stitches for what they are as they face you, knitting the knits, and purling the purls, but keep an eye on the slip stitches for a neat selvedge.

- Work in ribbing for ½″.

- ***Stop*** at the beginning of an outside row.

The Buttonholes:

- On this next outside row, work a buttonhole in the ribbing. Refer to Buttonholes, p. 18.

The Cardigan Sweater. *Worked in a lightish gray medium weight wool, this cardigan sweater is a match for its handwoven skirt fabric. Its border is worked with The Twisted Rib to coordinate with the body and sleeve ribbings. Seamline E enhances the yoke, and its "feathers" complement the twisted knit stitches of the ribbing.*

For a woman's sweater—work the buttonhole at the beginning of this row.

For a man's sweater—work the buttonhole at the end of this row.

- Continue the ribbing, and work one more buttonhole ½ " before you intend to stop.
- Then, work the ribbing to within one row of the desired depth.
- ***Stop*** at the beginning of an outside row.
- On this last outside row of ribbing, increase the number of body stitches by 10%, spacing them evenly between the borders. The number of stitches on the needle should equal the Key Number plus 12.

The Body:

The body of the sweater starts on an inside row.

- Change to the body size needle, and continue the Cardigan Border on the 6 stitches at each end of the needle. If you are working in stockinette stitch, purl the stitches between the borders for this inside row. If you are working in a pattern, you are on your own.
- ***Stop*** at the beginning of the next outside row.

To position the right and left seam line markers: refer to the *Key Number* of stitches. Do not include the 12 Cardigan Border stitches. These are excess to the front—6 each side. When the sweater is completed, on the body, and buttoned, the 6 border stitches overlap. Indeed, the front of the sweater then has 6 more stitches than the back; it needs them. For the sweater is a cardigan, most likely to be worn over something; the extra 6 stitches provide a better fit.

- Therefore, divide the *Key Number* by 2 to find the number of stitches in the back and the front. Then, divide the front by 2 to find each side front.
- As you work this next outside row, put a marker at the side seams. Remember do not start counting the front stitches until you pass the Cardigan Border.
- Continue working back and forth on the needle, keeping the first and last 6 stitches in Cardigan Border, ***and,*** continue the button-holes. About 3 " above the ribbing, ***stop*** at the beginning of an outside row.

Check Point:

Slip one-half the stitches onto a spare circular needle. This move opens the sweater to its full width. Check your gauge. In a cardigan sweater, there is less chance of a gauge change as the sweater is worked back and forth as was the gauge sample. Measure the full width of the body and if in doubt, wrap the piece around you. Remember the ribbing is still holding the body in somewhat.

- If all is well, slip the stitches back on the body needle, and work to the underarm.

The Cardigan Jacket. *A hairy Karakul handspun would have no business calling itself a sweater, so jacket, it is; this is truly a case of the yarn leading the way. Worked in Garter Stitch Rib (Row 1—K3, P3; Row 2—K), the jacket is reversible, your choice of in or out. The body starts directly with the Key Number of Stitches, and is not ribbed. The sleeves start with almost their full complement of upperarm stitches, and are worked with a K3, P3, rib for a cuff that automatically widens when the Garter Stitch Rib pattern takes over. The neck is high and ribbed with K3, P3; it is simply worked straight up a few more inches than is usual. With its matching Beaded Rib Scarf in place, the jacket certainly provides a snug, warm, shelter.*

The Cardigan—Chanel Style. *This sweater, sans buttons, features stripes of leftover handspun in natural shades from various and assorted black sheep fleeces. The body and the sleeves progressed simultaneously to ensure the stripe sequence of each section—a good idea when working with small amounts of scrap yarn. The extra length for the sleeve was accounted for with two extra stripes at the upperarm. Then all was in order again from the joining round up.*

- *Stop* at the beginning of an outside row. Do not break the body yarn. Start the sleeves with a new ball.

The Sleeves:
- Refer to the Basic Sweater.
- Work the sleeves to the underarm.

Joining—Sleeve Preparation:
- Refer to the Basic Sweater.

Joining—Body Preparation:
The *left* and *right* underarm: the seamline is the center of the underarm stitches; one-half are to the right, one-half are to the left. Run a scrap yarn through the underarm stitches at each side of the body. Tie loosely. The underarm stitches at each side of the body remain on both the scrap and the needle for the moment.

The Joining Row:
- Work the outside row to the right underarm stitches.
- Remove the left needle from the underarm stitches.
- Refer to the Joining Round of the Basic Sweater and attach the sleeves to the body.
- Work to the end of the outside row.
- Work the inside row.
- *Stop. Read.*
- Continue working back and forth on the needle, keeping the first and last 6 stitches in Cardigan Border, **and,** after the straight 1½″, start the decreases at the raglan seamlines.
- Work until 20 or 21 stitches remain to be decreased on each sleeve.
- *Stop* at the beginning of an outside row.

The Neck Shaping and the Neck Ribbing:
Refer to the Placket Neck.

The Laced Cardigan

- Work a buttonhole at each end of the needle using the substitute beginning and ending of Row 1 the desired number of times, at appropriate intervals.

The V-Neck Cardigan

Decision Point:
- Work the Cardigan Sweater to the start of the first raglan decrease row.
- *Stop. Read. Find a pencil.*
One stitch is decreased at the neck edges every other outside row, or every 4th row—however you want to think it. You must figure how many times to work the neck edge decreases:

Count the number of stitches in the right front. Do not include the 6 stitch border in this count. Count the number of stitches on one sleeve. Divide by 2, subtract the one-half sleeve from the right

The Laced Cardigan. *Knit of a lightweight 2-ply wool, this sweater, thought knit as a cardigan, will most likely go through life worn as a pullover. Worked with a buttonhole in each front border, it is laced like a shoe with Knitted Cord—all 80" of it. The otherwise plain yoke is shaped with Seamline D for a decorative, "feathery" touch.*

The V-Neck Cardigan. *Fibonacci directed the placement of the purl rows in this cotton and linen V-Neck cardigan. Worked on the outside of the fabric, they circle around the body and the sleeves, leaving his sequence between them in plain stockinette. The sweater is pictured here with its matching "scarf"—the remains of its original reject ribbing.*

front. The difference is the number of times to decrease at each neck edge. Once the excess number of stitches on each side front are decreased at the neck edge, discontinue the neck edge decreases. The remaining front stitches are decreased at the raglan seam line. Keep a careful count of the number of times (or stitches), that you decrease at the neck edge. If you decrease too many, you will run out of front stitches before the sleeve is gone. If you decrease too few, you will have front stitches remaining after the sleeve is gone. The sleeve stitches and the front stitches must disappear at the same time.

- On this next outside row, and every other outside row thereafter for as many times as necessary, work a decrease at the neck edges, **and** start the raglan seamline decreases:
- Start and end the neck edge decrease rows:

    Work the first 6 stitches in Cardigan Border, *K2tog.*, work to within the last 8 stitches, *SSK,* work the last 6 stitches in Cardigan Border.

    As the raglan seam line decreases are worked every 4th row for a while, and the neck edge decreases are worked every 4th row, combining them in this outside row starts you off in orderly fashion, and gives you 3 straight rows to follow. Once the raglan seam line decreases start their every other row sequence, this respite of 3 straight rows will end.

- Continue working the raglan seam line decreases in their proper order, and the neck edge decreases every 4th row as many times as necessary until the seam lines come together and the sleeves are gone. Do not decrease into the Cardigan Border stitches.
- ***Stop*** at the beginning of an outside row.
- Work the first 6 stitches in Cardigan Border, then slip them onto a holder.
- Bind off all the neck stitches, loosely, to within the last 6 stitches.
- With double-points, work back and forth over the last 6 stitches of Cardigan Border until the strip is long enough to reach the center of the back of the neck.
- Slip the first 6 stitches of Cardigan Border from the holder, and with double-points work the strip until it is long enough to reach the center of the back of the neck.
- Sew the border strips to the bound-off neck edge, and sew or graft the 6 stitches to each other at the center of the back of the neck. If you opt to graft, treat the 6 stitches as 3; in other words, graft the 6 two at a time, scooping a purl with a knit. True, this double-dip grafting will not be perfect, but to graft the 6 singly will spread them to full width. Grafting them two at a time preserves the ribbing with its hidden purls.

The Reversible Sweater

Pattern Stitch: K7, P1, or, P7, K1. The sweater may be worked, or worn, on either side. The directions are for P7, K1. Reverse the knits and purls if you go the K7, P1 route.

• Work a gauge sample in the pattern stitch.
• Determine the Key Number of Stitches. The Key Number will most likely have to be adjusted. Follow closely: the pattern is a multiple of 8 stitches. **But,** you must have an equal number of "8's" in the front and back sections of the sweater in order that the P1 (or, K1) is positioned at the side seams. Therefore, divide the Key Number by 8, and adjust until the quotient is an *even* number.

For example:

Key Number = 220

÷ by 8 = 27, plus a remainder of 4.

$$8\overline{\smash{\big)}\,220} \\ \underline{16} \\ 60 \\ \underline{56} \\ 4$$

with quotient 27.

You might be tempted to adjust down by 4 stitches to 216, rather than up to 224. Yes, 8 divides into 216, 27 times, **but** 27 is not an *even* number. You would end up with either 13 "8's" in the front of the sweater and 14 "8's" in the back, or vice versa. Which is why the quotient figure must be an even number. Adding 4 stitches to 220 sums up to 224—which divided by 8, equals a quotient of 28—an *even* number, and the front and the back will each have 14 "8's".

This is a large multiple with which to deal. Use your own best judgement whether to add or subtract to adjust your Key Number. Use the adjusted Key Number for all other figuring.

The Body Ribbing:

Determine your number of ribbing stitches. Key Number minus 10%. Adjust, if necessary, for your ribbing pattern.

• Using a 24″ circular ribbing size needle, work the body ribbing to the desired depth—minus 1 round.
• On the last round of ribbing, increase to the Key Number of body stitches. **Stop** at the right seamline.
• Count to be sure you have increased to the correct multiple.

The Body:

• Change to a 24″ body size needle, and starting at the right seamline marker, commence the pattern—either K7, P1; or P7, K1.
• Work the body to the underarm. Do not break the body yarn.

The Sleeve Ribbing:

Determine the number of ribbing stitches. 20% of the Key Number. Adjust, if necessary, for your ribbing pattern.

• Using 4 double-points in ribbing size, work the sleeve ribbing to the desired depth—minus 1 round.
• **Stop** at the seamline. **Read.**

The Sleeves:

Determine the number of upperarm stitches. 33% of the Key Number, plus 1″. Adjust, if necessary, to a multiple of 8. This math is easier—the quotient does not have to be an even number. Any number that 8 will go into without a remainder will do. Subtract the number of stitches on the needles for the ribbing from the number you eventually need for the upperarm. The difference is the number of stitches to increase before the upperarm.

- **For a full sleeve,** increase the needed number of stitches, evenly-spaced in the last round of ribbing. Change to body size double-points (and then to a 16″ circular, if possible), and starting at the seamline in pattern, work the sleeve to the underarm.
- **For a less full sleeve,** increase all but 8 of the needed number of stitches, evenly-spaced, in the last round of ribbing. Change to body size double-points (and then to a 16″ circular if possible), and starting at the seamline in pattern, work the sleeve to the elbow.
- **Stop** at the seamline.
- Work the next "7 purl" section as follows: P3, K1, P3, and work to the end of the round.
- **Stop** at the seamline, and remove the marker.
- On the next round, put the marker back after the "new knit stitch" in the purl section. You have created a new seamline. To increase the 8 stitches:
- Working the new knit stitch always as a knit, increase 1 stitch on each side of it every 6th row, 4 times. As the increased stitches come into existence, purl them. When the increasing of the 8 stitches is complete, the new knit stitch should have 7 purls on each side of it.
- Work the sleeve in pattern to the underarm, leaving the marker in place to identify the new seamline.
- **Stop** at the seamline. Break the yarn leaving a yard in reserve.

The Preparation for Joining:

This step requires less figuring than usual. Rather than finding the customary 8% of the Key Number, the underarm stitches for the reversible sweater must be 15. Otherwise, the vertical knit stitches will not come together in an orderly manner for the yoke decreasing.

Sleeve Preparation:

Full sleeve knitters—select a knit stitch near the seamline. Designate it as being the center of the underarm stitches, with 7 purls to its right and 7 to its left. Unknit any stitches involved. Run a scrap through the 15 stitches for the sleeve underarm.

The Reversible Sweater. *Worked in a lightweight 2-ply wool yarn, the reversible sweater is just the thing under a blazer or a raincoat. Shown here on its P7, K1, P7 side, the K1 makes a bold vertical statement. As well as being the focal point in the finished sweater, this K1 stitch exerts its influence and dictates the orderly construction of the sweater; it is the center of attention throughout. The K1 stitch centers the side "seams" of the body, the "seam" line of the sleeves, and works its way straight to the neck, centering the raglan seamline decrease. Would that all patterns behaved so well.*

The Reversible Sweater—The Knit Side. *Showing its K7, P1, K7 side, the reversible sweater is more subdued and tailored. Its purl stitch sinks to become the prominent knit on the purl side. So work it, or wear it, on whichever side suits your fancy.*

- Remove the needle from the underarm stitches.
- Repeat on the other sleeve.

   Less Full sleeve knitters—the new knit stitch is the center of the underarm stitches, with 7 purls to its right and 7 purls to its left. Unknit any stitches involved. Run a scrap through the 15 stitches for the sleeve underarm.
- Remove the needle from the underarm stitches.
- Repeat on the other sleeve.

Body Preparation:

   Locate the K1 at the *left seamline.* It is the center of the underarm stitches with 7 purls to its right, and 7 purls to its left. Run a scrap yarn through the 15 stitches for the left underarm. Tie loosely. These stitches remain on both the scrap and the needle for the moment.

   Locate the K1 at the *right seamline.* It is the center of the underarm stitches with 7 purls to the right of it and 7 purls to the left of it. Unknit any stitches involved. Run a scrap through the 15 stitches for the right underarm. Remove the needle from these stitches.

Here, you see an underarm view of the semi-fitted sleeve. Take note of the "new" knit stitch. The increases are made into the stitches beside it until the P7, K1, P7 pattern is regained. The underarm grafting is worked over this 15 stitch sequence, but on the inside, or knit side of the sweater. The P1 is indeed a misfit in an otherwise synchronized work.

The Joining Round:

- Refer to the Basic Sweater.
- At each of the 4 joining points there are 2 knit stitches side by side. On the round after the joining, knit the 2 knit stitches together. The remaining knit stitch is the center of the raglan seamline decrease. It will remain intact; work it as a **knit from now on.** On the next round, put a marker before or after it.

The Yoke:

   Note: the sweater is designed with a U-Neck. You may depart for other territories, on your own, if you wish.
- Work to within 2 rounds of the start of the raglan seamline decreases.
- **Stop** at the right front seamline.

The Neck Set-Up and Raglan Seamline Decreases:

- Count the number of stitches on one sleeve. Do not include the seamline knit stitch. Divide by 2, and add 4. The answer is the number of stitches to leave on the needle at each side front next to the sleeves.
- Run a scrap of yarn through the remaining center front stitches. Starting at the right front seamline, work to the center front stitches.
- Remove the needle from these stitches.
- **Turn,** and work the inside row reversing the pattern stitch to K7, P1, for this and every inside row. **Stop. Read.**

(As this is a plain vertical pattern, i.e., without cables, etc., a catch-up row is not necessary.) From now on, start all rows with a slip stitch for a chain selvedge:

Outside rows—slip as if to purl, yarn in front.

Inside rows—slip as if to purl, yarn in back.

The raglan seamlines are a combination of the purl decreases P2tog. and P1S1.

P2tog.—Purl 2 stitches together as 1. *Leans right* on the knit side.

P1S1—Purl 1 stitch. Return the new stitch to the left needle. Insert the right needle into the stitch behind it, and lift this stitch over the purl stitch. Return the resulting stitch to the right needle. *Leans left* on the knit side.

- On the next 4 outside rows only, work a decrease at the neck edge, *and* on this next outside row, start the raglan seamline decreases:

To take these 2 steps one at a time:

First, the neck edge decrease rows start and end:

Slip 1, P1S1, work to the last 3 stitches, P2tog., P1.

Second, the raglan seamline decreases:

Work to within 2 stitches of the K1 seamline stitch, P2tog., *K1, P1S1.*

- Work back and forth on the needle, working a neck edge decrease 4 times, *and* working the raglan seamline decreases in their proper order.

- **Stop** at the end of an outside row when the seamlines come together and the sleeves are gone.

The Neck Ribbing:

- Using a 24″ ribbing size circular needle in your right hand, purl into the left side neck chain selvedge, purl the stitches from the scrap (slip them onto a double-point), purl into the right side neck chain selvedge, and, purl the back neck stitches from the body needle.

- Count the number of stitches on the needle. Adjust, if necessary, in the first round of ribbing near a seamline.

- Work the ribbing loosely for about 1″.

- Bind off in ribbing loosely.

The Underarm Opening:

- Work the grafting on the knit side of the sweater. The center purl stitch will have to be happy grafted as a knit. Other than this 1 stitch that is a misfit on either side, the sweater is reversible.

- Tuck in all ends carefully—split the plies, and head the ends in opposite directions.

The Almost Sleeveless Sweater

Decision Point:

- Work the body of the Basic Sweater, the Crew Neck, to the joining round.
- Work the "sleeves" to the joining round as follows:
- Determine the number of stitches needed for the upperarm, 33% of the Key Number plus 1".
- Cast the upperarm number of stitches onto 4 double-points, or a 16" circular ribbing size needle.
- Work in ribbing pattern for the desired depth.
- Work 2 rounds of stockinette stitch.
- *Stop* at the seamline.

Joining—sleeve preparation:

- Refer to the Basic Sweater. The process is the same, even though the sleeve is practically non-existent.

Joining—body preparation:

- Refer to the Basic Sweater.

The Joining Round—and beyond:

- Refer to the Basic Sweater.

The Sleeveless Sweater

Though there are many variations of the sleeveless sweater, in general, its construction follows the basic premise that you work the Basic Sweater to the underarm, work the back stitches to the shoulder, work the front stitches to the shoulder, graft the shoulder seam, and rib the neck and armhole edges, or prefinish the armhole edges with a border of slip 1, P1, slip 1, P1. Worked in this sensible order, each step is an advantage to the next.

By working the Basic Sweater to the underarm, the garment is, to that point, seamless; it may be tried on; and, think of it this way, the sweater is half done. By first working the back stitches to the top of the shoulder, you can better visualize the eventual length and width of the front, thus making a wiser decision as to when and where to start the neck shaping. In fact, try on the sweater with the back in the front and mark the correct spot with a safety pin. Then, by grafting the back shoulder stitches to the front shoulder stitches, you are maintaining the sweater's seamlessness. And, if you choose to incorporate the armhole finishing while working the back and the front, two-thirds of the ribbing chore is thus eliminated; all that remains is the ribbing around the neck. However, more important than saving time, by pre-finishing the armhole edges you will know the exact depth and width

The Sleeveless Sweater. *The simplest of two-color knitting patterns mingle with plain stripes in this sleeveless sweater. Note that once the round knitting stops, so also does the two-color work—a simple solution for those who do not relish two-color knitting in the flat. The armhole is a hybrid—a combination of a bound off edge (the underarm stitches), and a pre-finished edge of Slip 1, P1, Slip 1, P1 the rest of the way around. Two-thirds of the "finishing" steps are thus eliminated, as the neckline is the only edge that remains to be ribbed. The yarn is a medium weight wool in natural shades of gray, brown and off-white. Its ribbing is laced with a Twisted Cord of two colors.*

of the armhole. The guessing game is over. For, as you know, no matter how deep an armhole looks unfinished, once ribbing is added, it shrinks in diameter, and when worn, the armhole may be binding with too high a rise. In the same vein, you also will be able to judge the shoulder width with more accuracy. Here again, no matter how narrow you make it, once ribbing is added to both sides, the shoulder may grow too wide. By pre-finishing the armhole, you must take only the additional width of the neck ribbing into consideration.

Whichever decision you make regarding the armhole, the beginning of the sleeveless sweater is the same for all. This particular version is designed with a U-Neck.

Decision Point:
- Work the Basic Sweater to within 2″ of the actual underarm if you intend to prefinish it, or, to within 3″ if you intend to add ribbing.
- Locate, and put markers at the right and left seamlines.
- **Stop** at the **left** seamline. Remove the marker.

    The back is worked to the shoulder first. The front is to be left "on hold." Therefore:
- Slip (as if to purl), the upcoming front stitches onto a spare circular needle. Remove the right seamline marker.
- **Stop. Read.**

    The next step is to locate, and isolate with markers, the underarm stitches. For the sleeveless sweater only, figure 10% of the Key Number of body stitches. This not only makes the math easier, but allows for a roomier armhole. Therefore:

    10% of the Key Number = _____ stitches for each underarm.

Now, divide the number of underarm stitches by 2 as each underarm is now divided; half the stitches are on the back needle, half are on the front needle. The underarm stitches _____ divided by 2 = _____. From each end of each needle, count in the one-half underarm stitches. Tie yarn markers (4) around the needle to separate the underarm stitches from the front and back stitches. To secure the front stitches, and to keep the ends of the spare needle upon which they rest out of your working way, fasten the ends of the spare needle together with an elastic. Using the circular needle, you will now be working back and forth over the back stitches only.

If you are working in a pattern, you may have to reverse your knits and purls for the inside rows.

Return to the left seam line and the body yarn.

The Cardigan Vest. *The amount of dark "champagne" handspun proved enough for a reversible U-Neck vest. Worked back and forth in a welt pattern of Purl 4 rows, Knit 6 rows, (reverse the inside rows), the fabric pulls up. It is a close relation of the fabric you achieved working Mary Thomas's Sampler B. Hence, the front edges of the vest are borderless to allow the fabric its freedom. The armholes are a hybrid, with the underarm stitches bound off, and the rest of the opening pre-finished. Its construction is the same as The Sleeveless Sweater, but worked in the flat. The shoulder grafting preserves its seamlessness.*

- *Turn.*

Decision Point: the Ribbed Armhole, or the Finished Armhole

The Ribbed Armhole

The Back:
- With the inside facing, *very loosely,* bind off the stitches before the marker. Work to the end of the row.
- *Turn.*
- With the outside facing, *very loosely,* bind off the stitches before the marker. Work to the end of the row.
- *Turn.*
- Slip 1 (as if to purl, yarn in front), work to the end of the row.
- *Turn. Stop. Read.*

The Armhole Shaping:
The armhole is further shaped by decreasing 1 stitch at each armhole edge on the outside rows only.
- Work the outside decrease rows as many times as necessary to narrow the back of the sweater to suit you, usually 6 or 8 times.
  Start and end the outside decrease rows:
    Slip 1 (as if to purl, yarn in back), K2tog., work to within 3 stitches of the end, SSK, K1.
  Start and end all inside rows:
    Slip 1 (as if to purl, yarn in front), work to within 1 stitch of the end, P1.
- Then, work straight to the top of the shoulder, omitting the decreases in the outside rows, but continuing to slip the first stitch.
- *Stop* at the end of an inside row. Break the yarn, leaving a good yard.
- Slip the remaining stitches to a spare circular needle, and secure the ends of the needle with an elastic as before.

The Front:
- With the outside facing, slip (as if to purl), the front stitches onto the body size circular needle. Tie the yarn into the first stitch at the right edge of the sweater.
- With the outside facing, *very loosely,* bind off the stitches before the marker. Work to the end of the row.
- *Turn.*
- With the inside facing, *very loosely,* bind off the stitches before the marker. Work to the end of the row.
- *Turn. Stop. Read.*

The Armhole Shaping:
The armhole shaping for the front is the same as for the back. Therefore, you will work the outside decrease row the same number of times, **but,** before the armhole shaping is complete, the neck shaping starts. Therefore:
- *Stop* at the beginning of the fourth outside decrease row.

The Neck Shaping:

Remembering that you will be adding an inch of ribbing to the armhole edge and the neck edge, determine the number of stitches for the shoulder itself, usually 2″ worth, but more or less, whatever you wish. The number of stitches for each shoulder = _____. To that figure, add the number of stitches remaining to be decreased at each armhole edge. Then, add 4 stitches for the U shaping at each side neck. The grand total is the number of stitches to leave on the needle for each side front.

- Tie yarn markers around the needle separating these side stitches from the center front stitches.
- Run a scrap through the center front stitches. Tie loosely.
- Work the 4th outside decrease row to the stitches on the scrap.
- Remove the needle from these stitches. They are to remain behind on the scrap for the moment. Slip the unworked front stitches beyond the scrap onto a spare needle, or a stitch holder. You will now be working back and forth over the stitches for the left side front only.
- Return to the left neck edge and the body yarn.
- ***Turn.***
- With the inside facing, slip (as if to purl, yarn in front), and work to the end of the row.

The Left Front:

- On the outside rows, continue working a decrease at the armhole edge as many times as is necessary to match the back armhole shaping, *and, on the next 4 outside rows only,* work a decrease at the neck edge:

  Work to within the last 3 stitches, SSK, K1.
- When the neck and armhole decreasing are complete, work straight to the top of the shoulder.
- ***Stop*** at the end of an inside row. Break the yarn, leaving a good yard. Slip the remaining stitches onto a stitch holder.

The Right Front:

- With the outside facing, slip (as if to purl), the right front stitches onto the body size circular needle. Tie the yarn into the first stitch at the neck edge.

  Before the neck shaping starts, this side needs two catch-up rows. Therefore:
- Work an outside row, slipping the first stitch as if to purl, yarn in back, and work the fourth decrease at the armhole edge.
- ***Turn.***
- Work an inside row.
- Now, start the next 4 outside rows only, slip 1 (as if to purl, yarn in back), K2tog., ***and*** continue working a decrease at the armhole edge as many times as is necessary to match the back armhole shaping.

- When the neck and armhole decreasing are complete, work straight to the top of the shoulder.
- *Stop* at the end of an inside row, break the yarn, and secure it.
- Slip the remaining right shoulder stitches onto a double-pointed needle.

The Shoulder Grafting

The Right Shoulder:
- From the back needle, slip an equal number of right shoulder stitches onto a double-pointed needle.
- Thread the reserved yarn through a Braidkin.
- Now, get this bit of contrariness: for grafting purposes, hold the needle with the back shoulder stitches nearest you; it is the Front Needle. Hold the needle with the front shoulder stitches furthest away from you; it is the Back Needle. The yarn is at the first stitch on the Front Needle. To begin the grafting process, it must be coming from the first stitch on the Back Needle, so as a preliminary step, slip the yarn through the first stitch on the Back Needle. Refer to Grafting, p. 54.

The Left Shoulder:
- Slip the left shoulder stitches from the holder onto a double-pointed needle.
- From the Back Needle, slip an equal number of left shoulder stitches onto a double-pointed needle.
- Thread the reserved yarn through a Braidkin.
- For the left shoulder grafting, the needles conform to their usage. Hold the needle with the front shoulder stitches nearest you; it is the Front Needle. Hold the needle with the back shoulder stitches furthest away from you; it is the Back Needle. The yarn is at the first stitch on the Front Needle. To begin the grafting process, it must be coming from the first stitch on the Back Needle, so as a preliminary step, slip the yarn through the first stitch on the Back Needle. Refer to Grafting, p. 54.

The Neck Ribbing:
- Attach the yarn at the left shoulder. Using a 16″ or 24″ circular needle (the length depends on the size of the neck), knit into the left side neck chain selvedge, knit the stitches from the scrap (slip them onto a double-point), knit into the right side neck chain selvedge, and knit the back neck stitches from the spare needle.
- Count the number of stitches on the needle. Adjust, if necessary, at the left and/or right shoulder in the first round of ribbing.
- Work the ribbing, loosely, for about an inch.
- Bind off in ribbing, loosely.

The Armhole Ribbing:
- Attach the yarn at the center of the underarm stitches. Using a 16″ or 24″ circular needle (the length depends on the size of the armhole), knit into the bound off stitches, knit into the chain selvedge around the armhole, and knit into the bound off stitches.
- Count the number of stitches on the needle. Adjust, if necessary, for your ribbing pattern.
- Work the ribbing, loosely, for about an inch.
- Bind off in ribbing, loosely.

The Finished Armhole:

The finished armhole is achieved by working a border of slip 1, P1, slip 1, P1, at the armhole edges. The border does not reverse its order; it is worked the same way at each end of the needle on both the inside and outside rows. The slips 1's are all worked:

Slip as if to purl, yarn in back.

To completely encircle the armholes with this border, stay here. If you don't consider a bound off edge a raw edge, go back to the Ribbed Armhole, bind off the underarm stitches, and return here for the Armhole Shaping.

For those who stayed: the slip 1, P1, slip 1, P1 border is established immediately and is used to cast off the underarm stitches. Therefore (to refresh your memory, you are at the left seamline with the body yarn):

The Back:
- With the inside facing, cast 4 stitches onto the left needle. You will be working back and forth over the 4 cast-on stitches to cast-off the one-half underarm stitches, as follows:
- * Slip 1, P1, slip 1, P2tog. (1 stitch of border with 1 underarm stitch). ***Turn.*** Slip 1, P1, slip 1, P1. ***Turn.*** *.
- Repeat * to * casting off the stitches before the marker. When the last underarm stitch is gone, work the inside row to the end.
- ***Turn.***
- With the outside facing, cast 4 stitches onto the left needle, and repeat * to * casting off the stitches before the marker. When the last underarm stitch is gone, work the outside row to within 4 stitches of the end, slip 1, P1, slip 1, P1.
- Work the inside row keeping the first and last 4 stitches in slip 1, P1, slip 1, P1.
- ***Turn. Stop. Read.***

The Armhole Shaping:

The armhole is further shaped by decreasing 1 stitch at each armhole edge on the outside rows only.

- Work the outside decrease row as many times as necessary to narrow the back of the sweater to suit you, usually 6 or 8 times. Start and end the outside decrease rows:

    Slip 1, P1, slip 1, P1, K2tog., work to within 6 stitches of the end, SSK, slip 1, P1, slip 1, P1.

    Start and end all inside rows:

    Slip 1, P1, slip 1, P1, work to within 4 stitches of the end, slip 1, P1, slip 1, P1.

- Then, work straight to the top of the shoulder, omitting the decreases in the outside rows.
- *Stop* at the end of an inside row. Break the yarn leaving a good yard.
- Slip the remaining stitches to a spare circular needle, and secure the ends with an elastic as before.

The Front:

Those who opted to bind off the underarm stitches may depart for the front of the Ribbed Armhole and return for the Armhole Shaping. All others:

- With the outside facing, slip the front stitches onto the body size circular needle. Tie the yarn into the first stitch at the right edge of the sweater.
- With the outside facing, cast 4 stitches onto the left needle, and repeat * to * casting off the stitches before the marker. When the last underarm stitch is gone, work the outside row to the end.
- *Turn.*
- With the inside facing, cast 4 stitches onto the left needle, and repeat * to * casting off the stitches before the marker. When the last underarm stitch is gone, work the inside row to within 4 stitches of the end, slip 1, P1, slip 1, P1.
- *Turn.*

The Armhole Shaping:

The armhole shaping for the front is the same as for the back. Therefore, you will work the outside decrease row the same number of times, *but,* before the armhole shaping is complete, the neck shaping starts. Therefore:

- Stop at the beginning of the fourth outside decrease row.

The Neck Shaping:

Remembering that you will be adding an inch of ribbing to the neck edge only, determine the number of stitches for the shoulder itself, usually 3″ worth, but more or less, whatever you wish. The number of stitches for each shoulder = _____. To that figure add the number of stitches remaining to be decreased at each armhole edge. Then, add 4 stitches for the U shaping at each side neck.

The grand total is the number of stitches to leave on the needle for each side front.

- Tie yarn markers around the needle separating these side stitches from the center front stitches.
- Run a scrap through the center front stitches. Tie loosely.
- Work the 4th outside decrease row to the stitches on the scrap.
- Remove the needle from these stitches. They are to remain behind on the scrap for the moment.
- Slip the unworked front stitches beyond the scrap onto a spare needle, or a stitch holder. You will now be working back and forth over the stitches for the left side front only.
- Return to the left neck edge and the body yarn.
- *Turn.*
- With the inside facing, slip 1 (as if to purl, yarn in front), and work to the end of the row.

The Left Front:

- On the outside rows, continue the slip 1, P1, slip 1, P1 border, and continue working a decrease at the armhole edge as many times as is necessary to match the back armhole shaping, *and, on the next 4 outside rows only,* work a decrease at the neck edge:

   Work to within the last 3 stitches, SSK, K1.

   On the inside rows, slip the first stitch as if to purl, yarn in front, and continue the slip 1, P1, slip 1, P1 border at the armhole edge.
- When the neck and armhole decreasing are complete, work straight to the top of the shoulder.
- *Stop* at the end of an inside row. Break the yarn leaving a good yard. Slip the remaining stitches onto a stitch holder.

The Right Front:

- With the outside facing, slip the right front stitches onto the body size circular needle. Tie the yarn into the first stitch at the neck edge. Before the neck shaping starts, this side needs two catch-up rows.
- Therefore, work this outside row:
   Slip 1 (as if to purl, yarn in back), work to within the last 6 stitches, SSK (the fourth armhold decrease), slip 1, P1, slip 1, P1.
- *Turn.*
- Work the inside row, and all remaining inside rows: slip 1, P1, slip 1, P1, work to within 1 stitch of the end, P1.
- *Turn.*
- Now, *start the next 4 outside rows only,* slip 1 (as if to purl, yarn in back), K2tog., and continue working a decrease at the armhole edge as many times as is necessary to match the back armhole shaping, and continue the slip 1, P1, slip 1, P1 border at the armhole edge.

- When the neck and armhole decreasing are complete, work straight to the top of the shoulder.
- **Stop** at the end of an inside row. Break the yarn, and secure it. Slip the remaining right shoulder stitches onto a double-pointed needle.

The Shoulder Grafting:

- Refer to Grafting for the Ribbed Armhole for the needle set-up. In the actual grafting process, treat the 4 stitch slip 1, P1, slip 1, P1, border as 2 stitches. That is, graft a slip 1 and a P1 as one stitch.

The Neck Ribbing:

- Refer to the Neck Ribbing for the Ribbed Armhole.

The Armhole Finishing:

- Sew the edges of the 4 cast-on stitches at the center of the underarm to each other. (Don't tell anybody.)

The Reversible Vest. *The Waved Welt produces a rippled backdrop for a handspun yarn of light gray wool mixed and carded with a creamy off-white. Having less pull-up than a true welt pattern, the waved welt allows the vest's front edges to be trimmed with Cardigan Border. The armholes are hybrid with the underarm stitches bound off, and pre-finished the rest of the way around. The shoulder stitches are grafted, the back to the front, thus the vest is reversible; the same on the inside as the out.*

The Sweatshirt Pocket

Decision Point:

- Work the Basic Sweater, the Crew Neck, to 5″ or 6″ above the ribbing for an adult, 3″ or 4″ above the ribbing for a child. The pocket is centered in the front of the sweater 3″ from the right and left seamlines for an adult. (For a small child, figure 2″ from the seamlines.) Translate stitches into inches according to your gauge:

    3″ equals _____ stitches.

    You must have markers at both the right and the left seamlines.
- *Stop* at the *left* seamline after working to the desired depth.

The Set-Up:

From the *right* seamline, *count* in towards the front of the sweater a number of stitches equal to 3″.

- Tie a yarn marker around the needle.
- Trace the next stitch down to the row above the ribbing.
- Tie a yarn marker through the stitch.
- Starting at the *left* seamline, work in towards the front of the sweater a number of stitches equal to 3″.
- *Stop.* Do not break the body yarn.
- Trace the next stitch down to the row above the ribbing.
- Working toward the left, slide a fine needle under one-half of each stitch, ending with the marked stitch.
- Connect a new ball of yarn to the first stitch on the right end of the fine needle.
- With a body size needle, knit the stitches from the fine needle—it may be easier to knit them out through the back.
- Put the fine needle aside. It has done its job.
- *Turn* your work.
- Using body size needles, purl across the row.
- *Stop. Read.*
- Continue working back and forth on the pocket flap, and work the first and last 6 stitches on the needle in Cardigan Border. This border provides a neat, firm selvedge for the pocket and will stand up to the wear of hands in and out. The pocket may be buttoned on the sides if you wish. When the pocket flap is halfway to the body needle, work a buttonhole at each end of the flap on an outside row.
- Continue working back and forth until the pocket flap is as deep as the body; a row shy is better than a row over—don't give the pocket a head start on sagginess.
- *Stop* at the beginning of an outside row.
- Break the flap yarn, and secure it.
- Hold the pocket needle in front of the sweater needle. With the body yarn, and the body needle, join the pocket to the sweater by knitting together a stitch from each needle.
- Continue working the body of the sweater to the underarm.

The Sweatshirt Pocket—Variations

The sides of the pocket may be curved in to stay, or curved in and then back out:

Curved in to stay:
- Work a decrease at each end of the needle inside the Cardigan Border on every other outside row, or more often for a sharper curve.
- Start and end these decrease rows:
  Work the first 6 stitches in Cardigan Border, *K2tog.,* work across to within the last 8 stitches, *SSK,* work the last 6 stitches in Cardigan Border.
- You *must* keep track of the number of stitches you decrease.
- Then, before attaching the flap to the body, work the body in toward the front of the sweater a corresponding number of stitches. Otherwise the flap will not be in alignment with the body as the two pieces are joined together.

Curved in and then back out:
- Work a decrease at each end of the needle inside the Cardigan Border on every other outside row, as above, to the half-way point. Keep track of the number of stitches you decrease.
- Then, work an increase at each end of the needle inside the Cardigan Border on every other outside row an equal number of times in the last half. Start and end these increase rows:
- Work the first 6 stitches in Cardigan Border, *increase* the next stitch, work across to within the last 7 stitches, *increase* the next stitch, work the last 6 stitches in Cardigan Border. As you increased out the same number of stitches you decreased in, there should be no problem with the alignment of the flap to the body for the joining.

The Mushroom Cap

The mushroom cap is so named, as standing on its ribbing, it is like a mushroom; simply changing from K2, P2, to stockinette stitch causes the cap to develop as from a stem. The K2, P2, gives for comfort, and the cap fits most any head. You may use any yarn, and cap size is adjustable by changing the size of the needles. (For the cap you may gently toss gauge to the wind.)

Use the smallest needle for a small cap;
Use the middle needle for a medium cap;
Use the largest needle for a large cap.
The cap is blank, waiting for your design ideas.

Needles:	Size of Cap		
	Small	Medium	Large
Fine yarn —	#3	#4	#5
Medium yarn—	#5	#6	#7
Heavy yarn —	#8	#10	#10½

- Onto a 16″ circular needle, cast:
  Fine yarn —120 stitches
  Medium yarn—96 stitches
  Heavy yarn —80 stitches
- Work K2, P2, for 4″, more or less.
- Knit around, for 4″, more or less.
- Try the cap on. Start to decrease when there is not too much left of your head to cover; there are 13 more rounds to the top.
- Put a marker on the needle at the seamline. Start the decrease rounds at the marker.
- Decreases:
  Round 1 —Knit 6, knit 2tog., around.
  Round 2 —Knit—and all other even numbered rounds.
  Round 3 —Knit 5, knit 2tog., around.
  Round 5 —Knit 4, knit 2tog., around. Change to double-points.
  Round 7 —Knit 3, knit 2tog., around.
  Round 9 —Knit 2, knit 2tog., around.
  Round 11—Knit 1, knit 2tog., around.
  Round 13—Knit 2tog., around.
- Endings:
  1. Break the yarn, and run it through the remaining stitches; pull them gently together, and secure. Add pompom or tassel.
  2. Continue decreasing to 3 stitches, work a Knitted Cord loop, and hang.

The Beaded Rib Scarf

Fair Warning: once you knit this narrow, shortish scarf, you may never take it of—indoors or out. It sits well on, or under a blazer, or a coat; and in a cold house, it's wonderfully warm around the neck—especially in a soft handspun. The beaded rib pattern complements any sweater ribbing. The pattern is a multiple of 5, plus 2, **plus** 3 extra stitches at each end of the needle for a garter stitch border. The casting-on and casting-off are accomplished on fewer stitches than the scarf proper to avoid "fanned fringe."

The scarf may be made wider, or narrower, by increasing, or decreasing, in multiples of 5, plus 2. And, it can, of course, be longer, or shorter.

Beaded Rib* Scarf—a multiple of 5, plus 2, plus 6 (3 + 3).
- Use 2 double-points:
    Fine yarn —#3, or #4, or #5.
    Medium yarn—#5, or #6, or #7.
    Heavy yarn —#8, or #10, or #10½.
- Cast on:
    Fine yarn —34 stitches.
    Medium yarn—24 stitches.
    Heavy yarn —14 stitches.
- Knit one row.
- Knit the next row, and increase 9 stitches for a total of:
    Fine yarn —43 stitches.
    Medium yarn—33 stitches.
    Heavy yarn —23 stitches.
- Repeat Rows 1 and 2 for pattern.
    Row 1—slip 1 (as if to purl, yarn in front), K2, *K2, P3*, repeat
        * to *, end K2, K3.
    Row 2—slip 1 (as if to purl, yarn in front), K2, *P2, K1, P1,
        K1*, repeat * to *, end P2, K3.
- Work 42", more or less. (Keep a safety pin in the Row 1 side, so
  you will know where you're at.)
- ***Stop*** at the end of Row 1.
- Knit the next row, and decrease 9 stitches to your number of
  starting stitches.
- Knit one row.
- Cast off, treating the last 2 stitches on the needle as 1 to further
  refine and square the corner.
- Fringe is optional.

*Knitting Dictionary, p. 40.

APPENDIX

Sweater	Yarn Source	Content	Color
Front Cover			
Crew Neck with Stripes	Bartlett 2-ply Fisherman	100% wool	Oatmeal
The Laced Cardigan	Bartlett 2-ply Sport	100% wool	Oxford
The Sleeveless Sweater	Bartlett 2-ply Fisherman	100% wool	Lt. Sheeps Grey, Med. Sheeps Grey, Spice, Oxford, Natural
Pages 104-105			
The V-Neck Cardigan	Scott's mill end	Cotton	Beige/White
The V-Neck Pullover	Scott's mill end	Cotton	Off-white
The Open Raglan	Scott's mill end	100% wool	Off-white variegated
The V-Neck Pullover	Handspun New Hampshire fleece	100% wool	"Champagne"
The Striped Crew Neck	Scott's mill end	100% wool	Off-white
	Handspun Harrisville fiber	Camel Hair	Camel
The Sleeveless Vest	Handspun Harrisville fiber	Camel Hair	Camel
The Cardigan Vest	Handspun New Hampshire fleece	100% wool	"Champagne"
Candlelit Windows	Handspun Massachusetts fleece	100% wool	Dark brown
The Slit Neck	Handspun New Hampshire fleece	100% wool	Light gray
Pages 108-109			
The Twisted Rib Cardigan	Harrisville 2-ply	100% wool	Oatmeal
The Matching Handwoven Fabric	Harrisville 2-ply	100% wool	Oatmeal, Aster, Cinnabar
The Placket Neck	Handspun New Hampshire fleece	100% wool	Med. brown
The Reversible Sweater	Bartlett 2-ply Sport	100% wool	Lt. Sheeps Grey
The Camisole	Handspun New Hampshire fleece	100% wool	Med. brown
The Crew Neck	Handspun Vermont fleece	100% wool	Med. grays
The Cardigan Jacket	Handspun Karakul fleece	100% wool	Lt. brown
Pages 112-113			
The "Chanel" Cardigan	Handspun varied fleeces	100% wool	Assorted scraps
The Cardigan Vest	Handspun	100% wool	Gray/White
The Low V-Neck	Kiwi, Thorobred, Brushed wool	100% wool	Oxford
The V-Neck—Lace Edging	Bernat, Cloudspun	70% acrylic 15% wool 15% mohair	Peach
The Boat Neck	Handspun New Zealand fleece	100% wool	Natural and Sandalwood
The Crew Neck	Bartlett 2-ply Fisherman	100% wool	Indigo, Bronze, Lilac Heather, Burgundy Heather
The Dedham Bunny	Bartlett 2-ply Sport	100% wool	Natural, Indigo
Page 116			
The Turtleneck	Bartlett 2-ply Fisherman	100% wool	Lt. Sheeps Grey, Denim, Bracken
Ringing the Changes	Bartlett 2-ply Fisherman	100% wool	#1 Lovat, #2 Bracken, #3 Bluebell, #4 Denim, #5 Lt. Sheeps Grey
The Back Cover			
The Hooded Sweatshirt	Bartlett 2-ply Fisherman	100% wool	Lt. Sheeps Grey
The U-Neck	Bartlett 2-ply Fisherman	100% wool	Natural, Lt. Sheeps Grey

NOTE: *The spinning, dyeing, knitting and designing are the work of the author. The handwoven fabric was designed and woven by Nancy Fee. The cover sampler was knit by Anne Gould.*

SOURCES:
Bartlett Yarns, Inc. Harmony, Maine 04942.
Bernat Yarn and Craft Corp. Uxbridge, Massachusetts 01569.
Scott's Woolen Mill. Uxbridge, Massachusetts 01569.
Kiwi Imports, Inc. 45 Accord Park Drive, Norwell, Massachusetts 02061.
Harrisville Designs. Harrisville, New Hampshire 03450.

BIBLIOGRAPHY

Abbey, Barbara. *Knitting Lace.* New York: The Viking Press, 1974.

Adrosko, Rita J. *Natural Dyes and Home Dyeing.* Dover Publications, Inc., 1971.

Albers, Josef. *Interaction of Color.* New Haven: Yale University Press, 1975.

Chamberlain, John and James H. Quilter. *Knitted Fabrics.* London: Sir Isaac Pitnam and Sons Ltd., 1924.

Debes, Hans M. *Foroysk Bindingarmynstur.* Torshavn, 1932.

Dexter, Janetta. *Double Knitting Patterns.* Nova Scotia Museum.

Gombrich, E.H. *The Sense of Order.* New York: Cornell University Press, 1979.

Karush, William. *The Crescent Dictionary of Mathematics.* New York: The Macmillan Co., 1962.

Kiewe, Heinz Edger. *History of Folk Cross Stitch.* Nuremburg: Sebaldus Verlag, 1967.

-----. *The Sacred History of Knitting.* Oxford, England: *Art Needlework Industries Ltd., 1967.*

Knitting Dictionary. New York: Crown Publishers, Inc., 1970.

Kovel, Ralph and Terry. *The Kovel's Collector's Guide to American Art Art Pottery.* New York: Crown Publishers, Inc., 1974.

Latest Novelties in Fancy Work. Isaac D. Allen Co., (est. 1871).

New Grove Dictionary of Music and Musicians. London: Macmillan Publishers Ltd., 1980.

Nylen, Anna Maja. *Swedish Handcrafts.* New York: Van Nostrand Reinhold Co., 1977.

Prospect Yarn Manual. New York: Prospect Sales Co., Inc., 1923.

Roosevelt, Eleanor. *Topical Files, 1945-1962.* Box 4642, The Franklin D. Roosevelt Library, Hyde Park, New York.

17th Century Knitting Patterns. The Weaver's Guild of Boston, 1978.

Thomas, Mary. *Mary Thomas's Book of Knitting Patterns.* New York: The Macmillan Co., 1945.

-----. *Mary Thomas's Knitting Book.* Dover Publications, Inc., 1972.

Walch, Margaret. *The Color Source Book.* New York: Charles Scribner's Sons, 1979.

Walker, Barbara. *Knitting from the Top.* New York: Charles Scribner's Sons, 1972.

Whitney's Treatise. Boston: T.D. Whitney Co.

Williams, Susanne R. *The Scotch Wool Shop Book.* Haverford, Pennsylvania, 1943.

Zimmermann, Elizabeth. *Knitting Without Tears.* New York: Charles Scribner's Sons, 1971.

-----. *Knitter's Almanac.* New York: Charles Scribner's Sons, 1974.

-----. *Wool Gathering.* Sept. 1979.

INDEX